ISRAEL
LAND OF PROMISE
AND PROPHECY

ISRAEL
Land of Promise and Prophecy

David R. Barnhart

ABIDING WORD PUBLICATIONS
EAGAN, MINNESOTA

Manufactured by Viking Press, Inc. Eden Prairie, MN

PRINTED IN THE UNITED STATES OF AMERICA

TO MY WIFE, MARY
whose love and encouragement have
been a never-failing source of strength

and

TO MY MOTHER, HELEN
whose Christ-like guidance placed
me on the road to Jerusalem

Contents

Acknowledgments

I am grateful to Dr. Robert Lee and to Zvi Strauss for their invaluable assistance in editing this book; to Ellie Knutson who assisted with the maps and artwork; to Raymond Masillo and Compass Tours Inc. of New York for their quality tour arrangments in Israel over the past years; and most of all, to my wife Mary. Without her support and counsel this book would not have been written.

ISRAEL
LAND OF PROMISE
AND PROPHECY

Introduction

My love affair with the land of Israel and her people has developed since my first pilgrimage in 1970. In His infinite goodness, God has permitted me to return to Israel many times, taking with me hundreds of people with whom I have shared the momentous experiences of walking in the footsteps of Christ and other notable Bible characters. But most of my family, friends and acquaintances have never been, and likely never will go, to Israel. Those who have been privileged to visit the Holy Land know all too well that there is so much to see, so much to remember; it is difficult to absorb it all. For these reasons I determined to write about Israel, not just for those who are fortunate enough to travel there, but especially for those who have loved Israel from afar through the pages of Holy Scripture.

While the book contains many facts and much information, it has not been written with technical language nor intended to be the last word about the land, the people or the holy places. It is meant to be read and enjoyed by anyone, trained or untrained, who seeks a deeper understanding of the Bible and the ongoing drama of redemption unfolding in Israel.

It has been my experience that some guides and many guide books go to great lengths to describe places or events of the Bible but fail, in the final analysis, to convey the great spiritual implications inherent in them. Also, I have been saddened at times by the comments of persons who have been to Israel but failed to gain from the experience. They claim disappointment that the Holy Land has changed so much from the days of the Bible and that there are so many churches and shrines covering the holy places. While their concerns have a certain validity, they somehow have missed the im-

3

pact of a unique contact with history- a history which has dominated world attention from ancient days to the bold headlines in the morning newspaper.

The churches and shrines in Israel were not erected yesterday. Most stand today as they stood centuries ago. They testify to the various epochs of history, secular and sacred, which have influenced the course of humanity. At the very most, one ought to be deeply moved; at the very least, one ought to be impressed when walking, praying and worshipping at the same holy places known to an endless line of pilgrims, who through the centuries endured countless hardships to walk and pray among the hallowed scenes of Scripture. Presidents and prime ministers, kings and queens, the greatest and the least, from Saint Francis of Assisi to Billy Graham- all have been pilgrims to Israel. They have traveled to Israel to kneel at the places made holy by the King of Kings and the Lord of Lords.

Israel is the only democracy in the Middle East. Her people are far from perfection, but they are an inspiration to all who love liberty and to all who believe that freedom is worth more than life itself. Their presence in the land of their heritage is no accident. "God hath brought His Israel into joy from sadness." I perceive Israel today as a bright light in a very dark world; a shining testimony to God's faithfulness in never breaking a promise; a sign of hope that Jesus is coming soon.

"Why do you keep going back?" people ask as I return to Israel year after year. Little do they realize that I crave the next experience in Israel more than the last. Just about the time you think that you have *arrived* in your understanding of even a small detail in God's plan to bring us salvation, He opens another window to behold still more of His glory and grace. No matter how long you have studied God's Word, no matter how marvelous your walk with the Lord has been - there's more, there's more.

With great fondness, I recall my first visit to the house of Caiaphas during my fourth trip to Israel. Never did I expect to see or experience what awaited me there. A faithful reader of the New Testament, I had thought that I was well acquainted with the events surrounding Jesus' last hours prior to His crucifixion. It had been my privilege to walk the Via Dolorosa, to pray at Gethsemane, to climb the summit of Calvary and worship before the empty tomb. Like so

4

many others, I wept at those places where I recalled the Savior's love so freely given. But there in the subterranean rooms of Caiaphas' house, I saw the pit (mentioned in Psalm 88) where Jesus was kept prisoner overnight before his mocktrial and crucifixion. As I stood there in that huge hole in the ground, I was overwhelmed at the thought of Jesus, the Lord of life, being subjected to such humiliation. And He did it for me! "My dear God," I cried, "I don't know at all what pains you endured to win my salvation." To this day, I am more deeply moved at this site than any other, knowing that the half has not been told.

And so, my friend, if in any way this book brings you one small step closer to our glorious Lord, if it gives you one small measure of insight into His love for you, then my labor is greatly rewarded.

Soli Deo Gloria.
David R. Barnhart
Eagan, Minnesota
October 1988

HATIKVAH

The National Anthem

כָּל עוֹד בַּלֵּבָב פְּנִימָה	So long as still within our breasts
נֶפֶשׁ יְהוּדִי הוֹמִיָּה,	The Jewish heart beats true,
וּלְפַאֲתֵי מִזְרָח קָדִימָה	So long as still towards the East,
עַיִן לְצִיּוֹן צוֹפִיָּה,	To Zion, looks the Jew,
עוֹד לֹא אָבְדָה תִּקְוָתֵנוּ	So long our hopes are not yet lost —
הַתִּקְוָה מִשְּׁנוֹת אַלְפַּיִם,	Two thousand years we cherished them —
לִהְיוֹת עַם חָפְשִׁי בְּאַרְצֵנוּ,	To live in freedom in the land
בְּאֶרֶץ צִיּוֹן וִירוּשָׁלַיִם.	Of Zion and Jerusalem.

ישראל

ISRAEL

Important Dates
In Israel's History

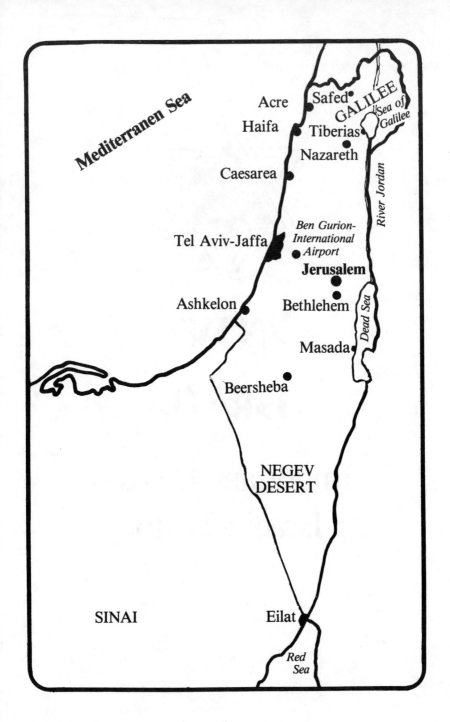

IMPORTANT DATES
IN ISRAEL'S HISTORY

164 B.C.	-	The Maccabees seized Jerusalem.
63	-	Pompey's victory established Roman rule.
40	-	Herod the Great appointed King.
4	-	End of Herod's reign and approximate time of Jesus' birth.
29 A.D.	-	Approximate time of Christ's crucifixion and resurrection.
66	-	First Jewish Revolt began.
70	-	Titus destroyed Jerusalem and the Temple.
73	-	Masada captured and destroyed.
132	-	Second Jewish Revolt began.
135	-	Bar-Kokhba defeated; Second Revolt ended.
312	-	Constantine legalized Christianity.
325	-	Queen Helena began extensive church building.
395	-	Byzantine rule began.
614	-	Chosroes II of Persia began reign in Palestine.
628	-	Byzantines regained control of Palestine.
638	-	Omar led Moslems to power in Palestine.
969	-	Egyptians began their rule of Palestine.
1071	-	Seljuk Turks invaded and conquered Palestine.
1099	-	Crusaders invaded and began 200-year rule.
1187	-	Saladin defeated Crusaders.
1250	-	Mamelukes came to power.
1291	-	Last Crusaders driven from Palestine.
1517	-	Ottoman Turks began 400-year rule.
1799	-	Napoleon's unsuccessful attempt to invade Palestine.
1897	-	World Zionist Organization founded.
1909	-	Tel Aviv, first Jewish city established.
	-	Degania, first collective settlement founded.
1917	-	British seized Palestine from Turks and proclaimed the Balfour Declaration.
1939	-	Britain's White Paper limited Jewish advancement in Palestine.

9

1947	-	United Nations voted to partition Palestine.
	-	Dead Sea Scrolls discovered.
1948	-	State of Israel declared; War of Independence.
1949	-	Israel admitted to United Nations.
1956	-	Sinai War with Egypt.
1967	-	Six Day War; Jerusalem reunited.
1973	-	Yom Kippur War.
1976	-	Raid on Entebbe to rescue hostages.
1977	-	Egyptian President Anwar Sadat visited Jerusalem.
1979	-	Peace treaty between Israel and Egypt signed.
1982	-	Invasion of Lebanon by Israel.
1984	-	Golan Heights annexed by Israel.
1988	-	West Bank and Gaza Strip uprisings.

ישראל

ISRAEL

An Overview Of
Israel's History

An Overview Of Israel's History From The Time Of Christ

Located on a small strip of land in the vast Middle East is the tiny State of Israel, with a population of 4,400,000 Jews and Arabs. Israel's presence among the sovereign nations of the world is nothing short of a miracle. Resurrected from her own ashes of humiliation, suffering, and persecution, Israel lives once more. Who would have believed that a nation destroyed in the first century and her survivors exiled throughout the globe could come to life again in the twentieth century with her religion, culture, and language intact? All attempts to rationalize the restoration of Israel or Jewish resilience after two thousand years of exile fall short without a full consideration of God's unbreakable promise to Abraham, Isaac and Jacob that He would preserve their land and heritage forever. Through the Scriptures, the land and the promise remained ensconced in the hearts of the exiled Jews from one generation to the next.

> If I forget you, O Jerusalem,
> may my right hand forget its skill.
> May my tongue cling
> to the roof of my mouth
> if I do not remember you,
> if I do not consider Jerusalem
> my highest joy.
>
> *Psalm 137:5–6.*

THE FIRST JEWISH REVOLT

A bloody revolt began in 66 A.D. as Jews sought to break the shackles of Roman tyranny. After a brief success, the rebellion was firmly crushed by the overwhelming might of Rome. First in Galilee, then in other parts of the rebellious nation, the Roman forces defeated the Jewish resistance movement with relentless brutality. In 70 A.D. the 10th Roman Legion, under the command of Titus, dealt a fatal blow to the Jewish revolt by destroying Jerusalem and the sacred Temple. A few survivors from Jerusalem joined a small remnant of Jewish partisans on King Herod's nearly impregnable desert-fortress, Masada. The final gasp of the doomed uprising ended with the fall of Masada in 73 A.D. when 960 Jews, including women and children, committed mass suicide rather than surrender to the Romans.

In the wake of their unspeakable reign of terror and destruction, the Romans left hundreds of thousands slain and the Jewish homeland in ruins. Nearly all the Jewish survivors were scattered as slaves or refugees among the nations of the world, although there was always a Jewish remnant in the land. In many of the countries where the Jews settled during the succeeding centuries, they were frequently segregated and persecuted in varying degrees. Yet, incredibly, it was this forced ghetto isolation and the severe persecution which were largely responsible for the preservation of the Jewish people, as well as the maintenance of their religion and culture. Beneath the yoke of persecution and exile, "Next year in Jerusalem . . . " became both their prayer and affirmation of hope.

THE PROMISED LAND AND ZIONISM

The Promised Land from which the Jews were expelled became known politically as Palestine. Many also called it "Terra Sancta," the Holy Land, since it was sacred to two other world religions, Christianity and Islam. During the long centuries which followed the Jewish diaspora, no independent nation ever emerged on the soil of biblical Israel. Instead, the land continued to be the conquered territory of many rulers: the Romans, Persians, Arabs, Seljuks, Crusaders, Mamelukes, Ottoman Turks, and the British.

Wave after wave of conquest brought more devastation to the land and to the people. Most of the forests, groves, and vineyards were destroyed. Fertile fields left untended became desert and swamps. Yet, even in this woeful condition, the land never ceased beckoning the Jews to return, reclaim, and rebuild. The summoning cry of the land was little heeded by world Jewry, however, until the latter part of the nineteenth century.

While in Paris in 1895, Theodor Herzl witnessed the public humiliation of a soldier named Alfred Dreyfus. His crime? He was a Jew. Through the Dreyfus incident, Herzl predicted that a new wave of persecution was about to descend upon the Jews of Europe. In a widely circulated pamphlet entitled *The Jewish State*, Herzl declared, "The Jews who will it shall have a state of their own." Herzl organized the first Zionist Congress at Basel, Switzerland, in 1897. There he presented his vision for a Jewish homeland in Palestine. Not many Jews were convinced at first, but Herzl never wavered. With unflagging zeal and determination, he traveled throughout Europe seeking to convince Jews that they should embrace the Zionist vision. At the age of forty-four Theodor Herzl died from a series of heart attacks in 1904, but his dream continued to live. The Zionist movement became both the inspiration and the driving force behind the establishment of the Jewish state. Theodor Herzl became known as the "father of modern Israel." Shortly after Israel was established, Herzl's remains were laid to rest in the land of his Zionist dreams. Today his grave is the centerpiece of Israel's National Cemetery on Mount Herzl in western Jerusalem.

Palestine was a very miserable place to live at the beginning of the twentieth century. Under Turkish rule since 1517, the land was poverty-stricken, devoid of forests, and plagued with malaria-infested swamps. There were few roads, no industry, and only the most primitive forms of agriculture. Yet by 1900, 50,000 Jews, mostly Zionists, were living and working in Palestine to reclaim the land. Wealthy Jews, including Baron Edward de Rothchild and Sir Moses Montefiore, purchased large parcels of land from the Arabs for Jewish development.

In 1917 Great Britain conquered Palestine, concluding 400 years of Turkish occupation. British rule in Palestine was often difficult for the Jews living there, but it represented a decisive turning point in

Jewish efforts to reestablish their homeland. A British document known as the Balfour Declaration set forth the concept of a Jewish homeland. Inspiration for this statement came from Chaim Weizmann, a British Jew who would later become Israel's first president. Weizmann, a scientist, labored much of his life with untiring energy seeking to influence world governments to recognize the Jewish right to a national homeland. Though he had no official office in any recognized government prior to Israel's statehood, Weizmann became greatly respected by various heads of government throughout the free world.

Britain's anguished rule over Palestine led them to change their minds regarding the proposed Jewish homeland. Instead of promoting a Jewish state, they sought to prevent it in every way possible. The infamous Palestine White Paper, produced by Britain in 1939 as an appeasement to the oil-rich Arab states, sought to limit Jewish immigration and Jewish ownership of land in Palestine. The White Paper was in direct conflict with the existing policy of the League of Nations' Mandate on Palestine which directed Britain to "facilitate the establishment of a Jewish National Home."

THE INFLUENCE OF THE HOLOCAUST

A unprecedented wave of persecution descended upon the Jews of Europe with the rise of the Nazis in Germany in the 1930s. Their civil and human rights were systematically revoked; their property was confiscated; and they became objects of public scorn and ridicule. Finally they were shipped like cattle to concentration camps throughout Europe to be worked as slaves and then exterminated. Of the 16,600,000 Jews living in the world at the outset of World War II, more than 6,000,000 were methodically murdered in Nazi death camps. Nazi crematoriums burned night and day, year after year. Yet, in spite of Hitler's great slaughter of the Jews, Britain continued to keep the doors of Palestine closed to further Jewish immigration. Even after World War II, when the full horror of the holocaust was known to the world and when hundreds of thousands of Nazi death-camp survivors were languishing in refugee centers of Europe, the British remained unyielding in their policy of limited Jewish immigration into Palestine. Sadly, other nations of the world were also extremely slow to admit the Jewish refugees. Shiploads of Jewish survivors endured long days and agonizing nights at sea on crowded boats, to be turned back from the shores of Palestine by the British. Only the clandestine efforts of Palestinian Jews and their supporters were able to penetrate British security by smuggling boatloads of Jews into Palestine under the cover of darkness. Because these vessels were often less than seaworthy, a considerable number of Jews died in their struggles to run the British blockade. Yet it is estimated that over 70,000 Jews were successfully smuggled into Israel by sea during the last years of the British Mandate.

ISRAEL'S STRUGGLE TO BE BORN

Weary of trying to keep watch over Palestine's Arab and Jewish inhabitants, Great Britain prepared in 1947 to relinquish control of the land by placing its custody into the hands of the United Nations. The Palestinian population at that time included 1,269,000 Arabs and 630,000 Jews.

After a long and difficult debate, the United Nations voted on November 29, 1947, to partition Palestine into two states, one Jewish and one Arab. In the U.N. partition plan, Jerusalem was to become an international city. The Arabs would have no part in the decision to divide Palestine. Immediately they set out to block all efforts to create a Jewish state. Jewish cities, towns, and settlements throughout Palestine were shelled and subjected to terrorism. The Jews responded to the Arabs' attacks in kind. Unbelievable bloodshed resulted on both sides.

Jerusalem, whose population had been predominantly Jewish for nearly a hundred years, was isolated by the Arabs and threatened with starvation. Eventually all roads leading to Jewish Jerusalem were blocked by the Arab forces. It looked as though the proposed Jewish state would never come into being.

Yet, facing certain war with five well-armed Arab nations but believing that the time was "now or never," the Jews of Palestine, through the voice of David Ben-Gurion, declared their state on May 14, 1948. The State of Israel was born struggling to survive. That very night bombs fell on Tel Aviv as the war machines of five Arab nations began their offensive to "drive the Jews into the sea."

17

THE WAR OF INDEPENDENCE

The Jewish nation fought bravely against overwhelming odds with only meager arms and limited manpower between May 14 and June 11, 1948. No country came to their aid. The United Nations watched and waited to see what would happen as the five Arab states attacked the newborn, sovereign State of Israel. Few expected Israel to survive. From within the borders of the new Jewish nation, thousands of Arabs left their homes and fled to neighboring countries. But the Jews had no place to flee. With their backs to the sea, they fought on. A truce went into effect on June 11. It is still a mystery why the Arabs agreed to the truce when they clearly held the upper hand in the war. But Israel took full advantage of the truce to purchase badly needed arms and war materiel from Europe. Money for these supplies came mainly from $50,000,000 raised by Golda Meir from the Jewish community in the United States. Though the Arabs were unable to improve their military status during the truce, and though they knew that the Israelis had greatly improved their military capability, they renewed the war on July 9, only to be soundly defeated in just ten days.

The War of Independence permitted Israel to enlarge her borders beyond the lines established by the U.N. partition plan. While most of Jerusalem was in Israeli hands, the Old City remained firmly under Arab control. Even the Western Wall, the holiest of Jewish sites, was on the Arab side of the city. In spite of armistice agreements signed by Jordan on April 3, 1949, which permitted access by all people to their holy places, Jews were prohibited by the Arabs from worshipping at the Western Wall for the next twenty years. East Jerusalem which was to be internationalized and the portion of land known as the "West Bank" which had been designated by the United Nations' partition plan as an Arab state were eventually annexed by Jordan.

Israel lost 6,074 lives in the War of Independence, nearly ten percent of her population. It was a tremendous price to pay, but the tiny nation endured. As a direct result of the war, 600,000 Arabs became refugees in nearby Arab countries. Except in Jordan, these Palestinian Arabs were never granted citizenship in any neighboring country. Most of the Arab refugees settled in camps where they would languish for decades. Children and grandchildren born in these camps would be raised in an atmosphere of hate and vengeance. Rather than assist these refugees to resettle in other Arab lands, the camps were deliberately retained by the Arab states as an embarrassment to Israel. Furthermore, the Palestinian camps were used as staging grounds for terrorist attacks on Israeli settlements and towns. These camps continue to be an injustice to both the Palestinian people and to Israel.

The fact that all the refugees in the Middle East in the late 1940s and early 1950s were not Arabs is often overlooked. Jews by the hundreds of thousands living in Moslem countries fled from bitter persecution and intolerance. In some Moslem countries where Jews had lived peaceably for centuries, they were suddenly stripped of all their property and expelled. Between 1948 and 1951, 754,800 Jews immigrated to Israel, more than doubling the population. How interesting that Israel could receive and resettle an increase of refugees greater than its own population, while 100,000,000 Arabs could not or would not absorb 600,000 of their own people. Over the next twenty-five years, Israel received 1,294,121 immigrants from various nations of the world, and almost half were from Moslem states.

WAR FOLLOWS WAR

Israel proposed repeatedly between 1948 and 1967 that the armistice lines of 1948 be made the permanent boundaries. Every proposal was rejected by the neighboring Arab states. During those same years, Jewish settlements in Upper Galilee were subjected to frequent shelling and terrorist attacks from Syrian guns on the Golan Heights. Terrorist attacks were also commonly carried out from Lebanon, Jordan, the Sinai and the Gaza Strip. The USSR supplied the Arab states with massive amounts of military equipment and supplies, fueling the fires of hostility.

In 1956 President Gamal Abdel Nasser of Egypt nationalized the Suez Canal and blockaded the Straits of Tiran to all Israeli shipping. In retaliation, between October 29 and November 5, Israel captured the Sinai peninsula and the Gaza Strip from Egypt. With assurances that both areas would be policed by U.N. forces and that Egyptian military would not be permitted in the Gaza Strip, Israel agreed to give up the captured territories. Regardless of those assurances, the Egyptians returned to Gaza just one week after Israeli troops withdrew. However, the U.N. Emergency Forces did remain in the Sinai, separating Egyptian and Israeli forces for ten years.

Tensions mounted between Israel and Syria throughout 1966 and 1967. Jewish settlements came under more frequent shelling from Syrian guns on the Golan Heights. In the spring of 1967, Syria, Egypt, and the Soviet Union spread false reports regarding concentrations of Israeli forces on the Syrian border. Several reports from United Nations observers indicated that no such Israeli concentrations existed. However, using these false reports as a pretext, Egypt placed 90,000 soldiers and 900 tanks in the Sinai. Nassar then demanded that all U.N. forces be withdrawn from the Sinai and the Gaza Strip. The U.N. troop withdrawal was swift and complete, leaving no buffer between Israel and the poised Egyptian forces. Again, Egypt closed the Straits of Tiran to all vessels going to or from Israel, in violation of international assurances that such a blockade would not be permitted. Other Arab states joined Egypt in forming an alliance, amassing troops along their borders with Israel. From May 15 until June 5, 1967, Israeli leaders waited in vain for the international community to convince the Arabs to halt their planned invasion of the Jewish state.

On the morning of June 5, the Israeli Air Force launched a surprise preemptive attack on the Egyptians, completely destroying their entire air force on the ground. Within hours Israel was in total command of the skies above the Middle East, as the air forces of Jordan and Syria were also largely destroyed. The ground fighting was fierce and costly on three simultaneous fronts. Five Arab nations attacked Israel, but in six days they were all soundly defeated.

On June 7, 1967, Israel overran the Jordanian forces in East Jerusalem and took the biggest prize of all, the Old City with its sacred Western Wall. For the first time in centuries, Jerusalem was a unified city under Israeli control. Soldiers and civilians gathered before the Western Wall, dancing and praying, crying and shouting with unbridled joy.

Israel also captured the Golan Heights in the north, permanently halting the shelling of Jewish settlements under their shadow. In the south, the Gaza Strip was in Israeli hands, together with the entire

West Bank. For the first time since 1948, Israel had a measure of security around her borders. Israel's losses in the Six Day War included forty aircraft and 676 lives. The Arabs lost 430 planes, 800 tanks and 15,000 lives.

Yet this humiliating defeat failed to sway Arab sentiment. A Summit Conference was held in August 1967 at Khartoum where they voiced anew their recalcitrant position: no peace with Israel, no negotiations with Israel, and no recognition of Israel.

THE YOM KIPPUR WAR OF 1973

Russia soon rearmed the Arab states surrounding Israel. Between 1971 and 1973, Israel offered to negotiate a peace settlement with her Arab neighbors and to establish new and permanent boundaries. But Jordan, Syria and Egypt talked only of the "full restoration of all Arab lands." On the Jewish Day of Atonement, October 6, 1973, Syria and Egypt launched simultaneous surprise attacks on Israel. Syria with 300,000 troops, 1500 tanks, 330 planes, and 32 anti-missile batteries moved against Israeli-held positions on the Golan Heights. Egypt with 800,000 soldiers, 1700 tanks, 550 planes, and 50 anti-aircraft missile batteries attacked Israeli troops stationed in the Sinai. Egyptian forces crossed the Suez Canal and seized a portion of the Israeli-occupied Sinai. Syrian troops temporarily regained a portion of the Golan Heights taken by Israel in 1967.

During the first two days of the war, Israeli troops stationed in the Golan and in the Sinai fought valiantly with support from the Israeli Air Force. Though outnumbered twelve to one and outgunned, the Israel Defense Forces (IDF) exacted a heavy toll on their enemies, but not without suffering heavy casualties themselves. Caught off-guard during the observances of Yom Kippur, Israel quickly mobilized her entire reserves and took the offensive. Soon the tide of battle was turned. Syrian and Egyptian forces were driven back. Israel actually invaded Egypt proper and surrounded the Egyptian Third Army in the Sinai.

In the Golan Heights, IDF forces drove the Syrians back so far that Israeli guns were in range of Damascus' suburbs. Only Russian threats and U.S. pressure prevented the victorious Israeli army from bringing the Arab powers to their knees.

When the war ended, Egypt's losses numbered 1150 tanks and 168 planes. Syria lost 1100 tanks and 222 planes. Human losses among the Arab states exceeded 14,000. Over 2500 Israelis lost their lives in the war, the largest number of casualties since their War of Independence. The Israeli people, stunned and grief-stricken, blamed the government of Golda Meir for not being properly prepared. The Yom Kippur War was won by Israel, but the price incurred was extremely high in lives and materiel. Also, the war devastated the nation's economy for several years.

THE SHAKY ROAD TO PEACE

The economy of Israel was not the only thing shaking following the Yom Kippur War. The political foundations also quivered. Yitzhak Rabin assumed leadership of the nation following Golda Meir's resignation as prime minister. Israel's morale had been badly damaged by her near defeat. The huge cost of the war created a skyrocketing rate of inflation. The unrest and political upheaval brought the Likud party to power with Menachem Begin as prime minister. Amazingly, under the administration of this "hardliner," Israel moved closer to peace with her neighbors than ever before.

THE VISITOR NOBODY WAS EXPECTING

November 19, 1977 was an unforgettable day in Israel. An Egyptian airliner landed at Ben Gurion Airport, just outside Tel Aviv. As the plane taxied to a stop, stairs from Israel's El Al Airlines were rolled to the door of the aircraft. Moments later, the figure of a distinguished and very proud man stood in the doorway. Egypt's President Anwar Sadat had come to call. Every political person who was anybody in the State of Israel stood below on the tarmac. Sadat had come to Israel in search of peace. Not since Bible times had the leaders of Israel and Egypt met face to face.

Sadat's decision to visit Israel was filled with irony. U.S. diplomats had worn themselves out with their "shuttle diplomacy," trying to convince Arab and Israeli leaders to sit down and talk. Then, in a live interview on a CBS news telecast, Sadat stated to Walter Cronkite that he was willing to travel to Israel in his quest for peace.

Cronkite immediately phoned Begin and urged him to issue a formal invitation for Sadat to visit Israel. The invitation was sent; the rest is history.

CAMP DAVID ACCORDS

In 1978 President Jimmy Carter hosted Menachem Begin and Anwar Sadat for peace talks at Camp David. It was a bold move which few expected would succeed. Face to face, hour after hour, they exchanged views. Finally, Sadat and Begin vowed to each other and to the world that there would be "no more war." They further promised to prepare a treaty of peace between their nations to end the state of war that had officially existed since 1948.

I had the privilege of being on the El Al plane which carried most of the Jewish statesmen back to Israel immediately following the talks at Camp David. When we arrived at Ben Gurion Airport, the Israeli leaders, including Moshe Dayan and Ezer Weizmann, stepped off the plane and were warmly welcomed by a large and friendly crowd. What an unexpected thrill it was to be part of that historic moment in Israel's history.

For their efforts, Begin and Sadat were awarded the Nobel Peace Prize in 1978. Rarely has anyone deserved it more. However, the peace they sought was still illusive. According to agreements reached at Camp David, the treaty was to be signed before Christmas of 1978. But many snags and obstacles in the final negotiations between October and December threatened to undo the entire peace effort. It appeared for a time that the treaty would never be completed. Each side blamed the other and insisted that no more compromises could be made.

Then, in March 1979, President Jimmy Carter traveled to Egypt and Israel to press to a conclusion the accords which had been so painstakingly worked out at Camp David. Traveling between Egypt and Israel, Carter met several times with both Sadat and Begin. The U.S. President addressed the government assemblies of both nations and pleaded that the peace process be completed. First Israel, then Egypt, accepted the compromises suggested by Carter. President Carter finally returned to Washington with assurances from both Sadat and Begin that the treaty would soon be signed.

On the White House lawn in Washington, D.C., March 26, 1979, the eyes of the world were riveted to the brief ceremony as Anwar Sadat and Menachem Begin signed the historic treaty ending a thirty-year state of war between the two nations.

Condemning the accords reached by Egypt and Israel, most of the Arab nations broke diplomatic relations with Egypt and tried to isolate Anwar Sadat from the Arab world. While the majority of Egyptians seemed pleased with Sadat's actions, a minority was fiercely opposed. In 1981 Anwar Sadat was assassinated by a faction of extremists. It is highly probable that the assassins were under orders from the Soviet Union, for Sadat had expelled the Russians from Egypt a few months prior to his murder. World leaders traveled to Egypt to attend the funeral of a man who dared to speak for peace in an atmosphere of hate and hostility. The treaty between Israel and Egypt continues to be honored by Sadat's successor, Hosni Mubarak. In keeping with the Camp David accords, Israel returned the Sinai, and the two countries exchanged diplomatic offices. While the relations between Israel and Egypt have never been overly friendly, the two nations continue to live in peace.

PEACE IN THE SOUTH AND TROUBLE IN THE NORTH

Though relations between Israel and Egypt greatly improved in the late 1970s, conditions worsened between Israel and her neighbors to the north, Syria and Lebanon. Jordan, while not officially at peace with Israel, has maintained a state of nonbelligerency and still permits travel between the two countries.

Expelled from Jordan and not too welcome elsewhere, the *Palestine Liberation Organization* reduced Lebanon to anarchy. Trained, armed, and financed by the Soviet Union, the PLO and other related terrorist organizations constantly harassed Israel. Their terrorist attacks were carried out not only in northern Israel, but also in various cities of Europe. Israel backed the Christian Militia in southern Lebanon, while Syria and Iran backed various competing Moslem factions in the country. Lebanon became a bloody combat zone as all vied for control of the war-torn nation. Every vestige of normal life was lost in the madness of internal war.

Then Syria entered Lebanon and became the dominant power. The PLO and other extremists were permitted to use southern Lebanon as a base for terrorist attacks against Israel and for shelling her northernmost towns and settlements. In March 1978 Israel invaded and occupied southern Lebanon, driving the PLO from the region. Jewish forces withdrew from southern Lebanon when the United Nations agreed to police the area. Unfortunately, the track record of the United Nations in the Middle East is very poor. The terrorists soon returned to southern Lebanon and resumed their attacks on Israeli territory.

In 1982 Israel was forced to invaded Lebanon again. This time there was no withdrawal. The shelling across the northern border was halted as the Israelis occupied the region. Also, Israel increased her support of the Christian Militia in southern Lebanon. During the invasion, huge stockpiles of weapons and armaments were discovered hidden in the region by the PLO. It took more than a hundred large trucks to carry this great cache of war materiel to Israel.

The war in Lebanon caused the badly inflated economy of Israel to worsen. The continuing loss of lives, too, prompted many Israelis to demand that their forces be withdrawn from Lebanon. This withdrawal was completed in 1984, leaving Lebanon's friendly Christian Militia in charge of the area. Today only limited numbers of Israeli troops routinely patrol the southernmost sections of Lebanon. Yet Lebanon remains a staging ground for terrorism. Hostage taking and hijacking are routine events in the region, with the encouragement of Iran, Syria and the Soviet Union. Though once forced out of Lebanon, the PLO has returned to carry on its program of Israel's destruction. Syrian forces also continue to occupy portions of the land, while Iran and the Soviet Union exploit the Lebanese tragedy.

40 YEARS AND GOING STRONG

In 1988 Israel celebrated 40 years of independence. There is no parallel in all human history to a nation developing so quickly into a world power. Israel's armed forces are by far the strongest in the Middle East. The Jewish nation is recognized the world over for advancements in agriculture, medicine and industry. Israel's agricultural insights are helping to alleviate starvation in areas of the world where water is scarce and desert is plentiful. Israel's deserts are in bloom as foretold in the Bible. So many flowers are raised in the Negev desert of Israel that they are exported to Holland, the floral capital of the world. Crops are harvested along the shores of the Dead Sea where nothing has ever been raised. Production records per acre are constantly being broken within the kibbutzim and farms. Israel now produces eighty-five percent of its own food supply. As new industries are established in the young nation, new buildings rise in the cities.

Israel's Arab population enjoys the highest standard of living among any of the surrounding states. Tension continues, however, between Arabs of the West Bank and Gaza and the Israelis. In late 1987 and 1988, a new wave of violence erupted as Arabs protested their treatment at the hands of the Israelis. Several of the Palestinians accused of promoting the uprisings in the occupied territories were deported to Lebanon. These deportations were condemned by the United Nations Security Council with the support of Israel's strongest ally, the United States. More than 250 Arabs were killed as they protested Israel's continued occupation of the territories captured in the 1967 War. The Jewish government is badly divided regarding the occupation of the West Bank and Gaza. Renewed calls for the annexation of the West Bank are frequently voiced by the "hardliners," while the moderates call for direct negotiations with the Palestinians.

The entire political scene on the West Bank dramatically changed in August 1988 when King Hussein of Jordan relinquished all claims to the territory and opened the door of political leadership in the West Bank to the PLO. This action prompted some Palestinian leaders to call for the establishment of a Palestinian state with a government in exile led by the PLO, or a provisional government led by local West Bank residents.

Just how the Palestinian problem will be resolved is anyone's guess. The PLO, refusing to recognize Israel's right to exist, wants a separate Arab state composed of the West Bank, the Gaza Strip and Jerusalem as its capital, all the lands taken by Israel since 1948. The Israelis have built extensive settlements on the West Bank for both security and expansionist purposes. Solutions are sure to be slow and painful for both sides.

Annually more than a million tourists visit Israel and are accommodated in some of the finest hotels and restaurants in the world. Tourism is Israel's number one industry, and visitors, whatever their faith may be, have complete access to all the holy places. Israel is the only democracy in the Middle East in spite of her faults and failures. Though the nation has many problems, it is still the last, best hope today for many Jews who are persecuted in numerous countries of the world, especially behind the Iron Curtain.

Standing in Jerusalem is Yad Vashem, a memorial to the six million Jews who were so cruelly murdered by the Nazis during World War II. Truly this monument symbolizes the inner strength and determination of the Jewish people to take the worst the world could hurl at them and not only to survive but also to build a strong and independent nation where human freedom and dignity are honored.

ישראל

ISRAEL

The Old City
Of Jerusalem

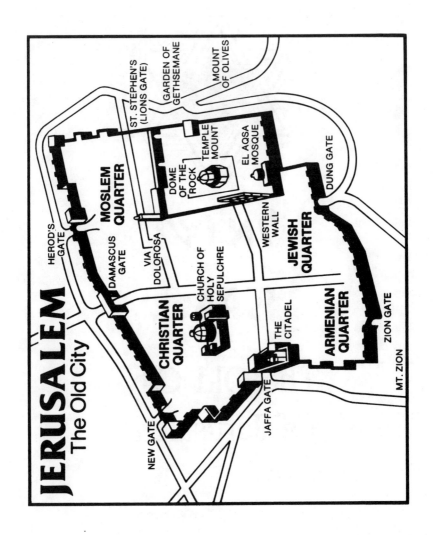

JERUSALEM
The Old City

NEW GATE

CHRISTIAN QUARTER

CHURCH OF HOLY SEPULCHRE

JAFFA GATE

THE CITADEL

ARMENIAN QUARTER

ZION GATE

MT. ZION

HEROD'S GATE

DAMASCUS GATE

VIA DOLOROSA

MOSLEM QUARTER

WESTERN WALL

JEWISH QUARTER

DOME OF THE ROCK

TEMPLE MOUNT

EL AQSA MOSQUE

DUNG GATE

ST. STEPHEN'S (LIONS GATE)

GARDEN OF GETHSEMANE

MOUNT OF OLIVES

The Old City Of Jerusalem

Few experiences equal the joy of seeing the walls of Jerusalem for the first time. Is there a more important place in all human history? The timeworn walls of the Old City still stand as majestically as they did centuries ago when some of the world's greatest warriors sought to conquer and possess her.

Jerusalem dates back thousands of years to Canaanite times. Abraham paid tribute to Melchizedek, king of Salem. Joshua successfully fought against the city as he marched to possess the Promised Land. King David captured the city from the Jebusites and made it his national capital. Under the reign of Solomon, Jerusalem's splendor was unsurpassed throughout the world.

While Jerusalem has known great moments of glory, it has also known the agony of war and destruction. All the glory of Solomon's city crumbled under the heels of Nebuchadnezzar in 586 B.C. when he not only destroyed the city and its Temple but also carried off most of the survivors to Babylon. The exiles from Babylon returned some seventy years later and rebuilt the Temple under the leadership of Zerubbabel. It is said that the old men of Israel wept when they saw the Temple of Zerubbabel, remembering the former glory of Solomon's Temple (Ezra 3:12). Following the Babylonian exile, the walls of Jerusalem were rebuilt under the highly skilled administration of Nehemiah. A small portion of this wall was uncovered in the excavation of David's City.

In 332 B.C. Alexander the Great included Israel in his empire. Then the infamous Antiochus Epiphanes came to power in 175 B.C. His reign of terror brought death to thousands of Jews and desecration to the Temple. As a result, a great rebellion broke out in 167 B.C., bringing to power a Jewish dynasty known as the Maccabees and their successors, the Hasmoneans. The Jewish nation knew relative independence under their rule for nearly 100 years.

But in 63 B.C. Pompey marched on Jerusalem in the name of Rome. The land remained under Roman authority for nearly 500 years. Herod the Great, having emerged as victor in a fierce struggle for power, was appointed puppet king of Israel by the Roman emperor in 40 B.C. Herod undertook a grander building program than had been seen since the days of Solomon. He strengthened and enlarged the walls of Jerusalem, building defense towers every two hundred feet. His masterpiece was the restored Temple which took forty-six years to complete. The population of Jerusalem at the time of Herod was approximately 100,000, often swelling to 500,000 during the great Jewish feasts.

Jesus Christ was born in Bethlehem, located just six miles south of Jerusalem, shortly before Herod's death. His thirty-three years were lived under the yoke of Roman oppression. When the Jews sought to free themselves from Rome's tyranny between 66 and 70 A.D., the entire country, including Jerusalem, was completely devastated. Vespasian crushed the revolt in the north and his son Titus completed the conquest of the Jews, including the destruction of Jerusalem. Josephus estimated that, of the 3,000,000 people living in Israel at the beginning of the First Jewish Revolt, 1,100,000 perished in Titus' siege of Jerusalem.

During Jerusalem's long ordeal, starvation became so severe within the city that the people resorted to cannibalism. When Jews were caught outside the city walls searching for food, their hands were cut off by the Romans, and then they were returned to the city to face a slow death by starvation or they were crucified. Titus' final assault on Jerusalem was accomplished by the construction of an earthen ramp against the city's northern wall. This same procedure was used to gain entrance to the fortress of Masada in 73 A.D. The final stand of the Jews in Jerusalem against Titus was made at the Temple. After crushing the last resistance, Titus walked about the Temple, then ordered its complete destruction, fulfilling Jesus' prophecy that "not one stone would be left upon another." Emperor Hadrian sought to "Romanize" Jerusalem in 135 A.D. After quelling the Second Jewish Revolt, he plowed the city with a yoke of oxen and then began to rebuild it. The name was changed to Aelia Capito-

A Hassidic man and boy in the Old City.

lina and all Jews were forbidden, under the penalty of death, from entering the city. The emperor also erected pagan temples on the Temple Mount and on various Christian holy sites.

Shortly after the Emperor Constantine came to power in 312, Christianity was officially recognized. He ordered the pagan temples in Jerusalem and other parts of the country to be destroyed. Then he sent his mother, Queen Helena, to search for the holy places from the life of Christ and to direct the building of churches on the various sites. Altogether, Helena was responsible for the erection of an estimated thirty churches and shrines in the Holy Land, including the Church of the Nativity in Bethlehem and the Church of the Holy Sepulchre in Jerusalem.

The Persians, led by Chosroes II, gained control of Jerusalem in 614. The Jews were highly cooperative during his military campaign, and as a result they enjoyed a measure of freedom for three years. Churches were destroyed and many Christians were put to death. Jerusalem returned to Christian hands for a second time, but in 638 the Arab forces of Omar captured the city and ruled until forced out by the Egyptians in 969.

In 1077 the Seljuk Turks were the next to take their turn in the conquest of Palestine. Stories regarding Turkish persecution of Christians and the desecration of holy places so outraged the peoples of Europe that the great Crusades were inaugurated by Pope Urban II in 1095. Godfrey de Bouillon led the Crusader armies to victory over the Seljuk Turks in 1099 and became ruler of Jerusalem. The walls of the city were restored once more, and scores of new churches and fortresses were constructed throughout the land. The Crusader reign, often brutal for both Jews and Arabs, came to an end in 1187 when they were defeated near Galilee by the Arab sultan, Saladin. For a time, he closed the Church of the Holy Sepulchre and imposed excessive taxes on the Christians. In 1189 Richard the Lion-heart joined forces with other kings of Europe to launch yet another Crusade. While they succeeded in capturing the port city of Acre, the Crusaders were unable to dislodge Saladin from Jerusalem. The second Crusade also ended in defeat. Although the Crusaders did manage to cling to several coastal cities for another hundred years, their power and influence faded. In 1250 the Mamelukes seized control of Palestine, and by 1291 the last of the Crusaders were driven from

Acre. The Mamelukes ruled the region until 1517 when they were defeated by the Ottoman Turks.

The 400-year rule of the Ottoman Turks did little to improve conditions in Jerusalem. Outlandish taxes on churches and pilgrims were imposed by the government. Control of churches and holy places was handed back and forth to the highest bidder; most fell into ruin from lack of repair. It was basically a time of insecurity and oppression. The general population of the country declined to perhaps as few as 250,000 in the early part of the nineteenth century.

The Turks' hold on Palestine was broken in 1917 by the British who governed the region until 1948 under a mandate from the League of Nations. At first the British supported the Zionist dream of a Jewish homeland in Palestine, but, as the years passed, their support turned into open opposition. In 1947 the United Nations voted to partition Palestine. The Arabs rejected the plan and immediately set out to remove the Jews from the entire region. When the War of Independence ended in 1949, the State of Israel was firmly established and much of Jerusalem was a part of the Jewish nation. But the Old City remained under Arab control and was later annexed together with the West Bank by Jordan. Jerusalem was divided by barriers and barbed wire until the Six Day War in 1967. Until that time, Jordan would not permit entrance to East Jerusalem or the West Bank from the territory of Israel.

The 2500 residents of the Old City's Jewish Quarter were forced to surrender during the War of Independence following a long and difficult siege. Leaving the shambled ruins of their homes, the Jewish residents were evacuated to West Jerusalem under the terms of surrender. Every one of the more than twenty-five synagogues in the Jewish Quarter was destroyed either as a result of the fighting or desecration by the Arabs, as were thousands of Jewish graves on the Mount of Olives.

Since 1967 Israel has rebuilt the Jewish Quarter in keeping with the Old City's architecture. While digging the foundations for new structures in the Jewish Quarter, many exciting discoveries from ancient times were uncovered and preserved. One of the most interesting parts of the Old City now lies beneath the modern buildings of the restored Jewish Quarter. There you can see the newly opened Herodian Quarter, a complex of buildings from the period prior to the fall

A graceful arch marks the site of the Hurva Synagogue in the restored Jewish Quarter.

of Jerusalem in 70 A.D., as well as an ancient wall from the time of King Hezekiah and a house destroyed by the Romans. The first-century house belonged to the Kathros family. The archaeologists uncovered information in it revealing the exact day, month,and year that the house was destroyed, the eighth of Elul, 70 A.D. Coins, furniture and pottery were also found in the house, as well as a spear near the outstretched hand of a woman.

Stepping through the gates of the Old City is like turning the clock back 2000 years. The shops and bazaars, the narrow streets and crowded houses, are like pictures of antiquity. Except for electric lights and television antennas on the roofs, there are few reminders of the twentieth century.

Shopkeepers eagerly welcome the thousands of tourists who walk the streets. Racks of clothing, stacks of leather goods, olivewood carvings, mother-of-pearl statues and jewelry are displayed on open shelves and in doorways. Each merchant assures the passers-by that he has the best prices and the finest merchandise available. Those tourists who actually stop and enter a store will likely be offered a cup of Turkish coffee and a very "special deal, because you are my friend." Often the bartering goes on in the street after a customer leaves the shop. Not until the Arab merchant is driven below his lowest price will he halt the negotiations.

Arabs in native attire, priests and nuns in religious garb, soldiers in uniform, handsome young people in modern clothing, all blend with the camera-toting tourists on the narrow and crowded streets of Jerusalem. Sweet aromas from Arab bake shops sometimes give way to the foul odors emanating from unclean streets. Fruits and vegetables are heaped high in the stalls, while fresh carcasses of sheep are hung in the open air.

Old City residents impatiently push their way through the crowds of ambling tourists and shoppers as they go about their daily chores. It is worth noting that approximately 30,000 people live within the walls of the Old City. Few cars or trucks are found on the extremely narrow streets, but once in awhile some do accept the challenge, creating no small amount of confusion as pedestrians scramble out of their way. Donkeys with heavy burdens are forced into the crowds, adding still more annoyance. Young Arab children with large trays of fresh bread precariously balanced on their heads move nonchalantly through the crowds without a crumb falling to the ground. Beggars of all ages are a common sight along the busy streets. Not as noticeable, but usually present lurking in the shadows, are the thieves and pickpockets.

The Old City is divided into four quarters- Jewish, Christian, Moslem, and Armenian. Each quarter is distinctive in its culture and traditions. Homes in the Moslem Quarter are often decorated with paintings depicting the required pilgrimage to Mecca.

A most worthwhile experience in the Old City is walking on the ancient wall itself. The ledge around the wall is fairly wide and not too difficult to traverse. Railings have been added as a safety factor. The scenes from the wall offer a view of Jerusalem unlike any other vantage point. The view from the eastern side of the wall is especially magnificent, giving one not only a unique vista of the Old City but also an unsurpassable panorama of the Kidron Valley and the Mount of Olives. Entrance to this section of the wall is located at Lions Gate.

ישראל

ISRAEL

The Gates of Jerusalem

The Lions Gate leading to the Moslem Quarter.

The Gates Of Jerusalem

THE DAMASCUS GATE, the most picturesque and beautiful of all the gates, built in 1542 by Suleiman the Magnificent, rises to a height of fifty feet at the center of the city's northern wall. Two towers flank its impressive arch, over which a message is carved that includes the words: "There is no God but Allah and Mohammed is His Prophet."

The gate's inner hall has a vaulted ceiling, and, for defensive purposes, two sharp turns are required before the city street can be reached. Visible below the present gate are the ruins of a second-century wall and gate, revealing the actual level of the street at the time of Hadrian. The older gate leads into excavations from the second century, while the main gate opens to the Moslem Quarter.

If Christ was crucified at the location of Gordon's Calvary, it is likely that He would have carried His cross through the existing gate at this location. It is also reasonable to assume that Paul left the city through the same gate when he traveled to Damascus to persecute the Christians there.

HEROD'S GATE, also known as the Gate of Flowers, is located on the north wall across from the Rockefeller Museum. The gate opens to the Moslem Quarter. Each Friday the area near Herod's Gate becomes an Arab market where sheep and goats are bartered and sold. At the time of Jesus an inner gate close to the Pool of Bethesda was called the Sheep Gate. How amazing that, centuries later, the same commerce takes place in the same general area.

THE NEW GATE, the third gate on the city's northern wall, is the most recently constructed. Built in 1889, it leads to the Christian Quarter and is located directly across the street from the Vatican's

Notre Dame hospice. Quite unimpressive in comparison to several of the other gates, it was sealed shut in 1948 by the Arabs, and remained closed until 1967 when Israel reopened it.

THE LIONS GATE, the only entrance to the eastern side, is commonly called Saint Stephen's Gate. Some traditions maintain that Stephen, the first Christian martyr, was stoned to death outside this gate (Acts 7:54–60). Two lions carved in stone on each side of the outer archway are the inspiration for its name. It was through this gate that the Israeli Defense Forces stormed the Old City on June 7, 1967. The gate gives direct access to the Moslem Quarter.

THE GOLDEN GATE, the Palm Sunday Gate, the Eastern Gate, and the Beautiful Gate are all common names given to one of the most impressive and important entrances to the Old City. Ironically, it has been sealed shut since the ninth century. Christ entered Jerusalem on His Palm Sunday ride through the Eastern Gate. The traditional Palm Sunday Road lies directly opposite on the slopes of the Mount of Olives, and Christian pilgrims often walk down that road to commemorate Jesus' entrance into the city one week prior to His crucifixion and resurrection.

The position of the eastern wall and the Golden Gate are likely unchanged from ancient times. Some archaeologists believe that portions of the present eastern wall may date to the time of Solomon, or certainly to the time of Christ. During biblical times the Golden Gate opened directly to the Temple Mount in line with an inner gate known as the Beautiful Gate. It is possible that this second gate was the location for the healing of the lame man by Peter and John (Acts 3:1-10). The present gate with its double portals and arches was built in the early Moslem period.

Ancient Jewish tradition, supported by Scripture, indicates that the Messiah will enter through this gate and begin His rule in Jerusalem. In an effort to prevent the Jewish Messiah from fulfilling this prophecy, the Arabs sealed the Golden Gate in 810. It was reopened by the Crusaders, but only for their Palm Sunday processions. When the Arabs regained control of Jerusalem in 1187, they sealed it up again. Except for a few brief intervals, it has remained closed to this day. Interestingly, the prophet Ezekiel foretold the sealing of this gate in the "latter days" (Ezekiel 44:1-3). As with the rebuilding of the Temple, might there not be a correlation between this gate's reopening and the Messiah's soon coming? If so, we would do well to keep our eyes on this "closed" gate.

As further insurance against the coming of the Jewish Messiah, the Moslems created a cemetery in front of the outer portion of the Eastern Gate "as a barrier of ritual purity." How awesome that all three of Jerusalem's faiths, in one way or another, are waiting for the Jewish Messiah to enter through this gate.

THE DUNG GATE offers the most convenient access to the Western Wall (Wailing Wall). Its rather uncouth name comes from ancient times when the gate's main function was to serve as a back door for the southside of the city. Refuse was carried through the gate to the Valley of Hinnom (Gehenna). The thoroughfare on both sides of the gate has been greatly improved by Israel in recent years, in keeping with the beautification of the entire Western Wall area. The area just inside the Dung Gate offers a commanding view of the recent excavations and discoveries at the southern end of the Temple Mount.

ZION GATE opens from the southwestern portion of the wall into the Armenian and Jewish Quarters of the Old City. It is known also as David's Gate because of its proximity to the Tomb of David on Mount Zion. Heavy fighting took place at Zion Gate during the War of Independence as Israeli forces endeavored to break into the besieged Jewish Quarter. Deep holes produced by the intensive shelling in 1948 and 1967 are still visible around the gate. The Jews of the Old City were forced to surrender to the Arabs in 1948 after all attempts by the Israeli forces failed to effect a rescue. Immediately after the unconditional surrender was signed, approximately 100 Israeli soldiers and 200 civilians, including fifty wounded, were taken prisoner. The other residents of the Jewish Quarter were permitted to leave through the Zion Gate. The Quarter was then looted and set on fire. Shortly afterward the gate was sealed shut by the Arabs. It remained closed until 1967.

THE JAFFA GATE gives access to the Christian, Armenian and Jewish Quarters; thus it is an area of very heavy traffic. An inscription above the gate reads: "There is no God but Allah, and Ibrahim

43

is his friend." The Arabs sometimes refer to it as the Gate of the Friend. One may also enter the Citadel of David from the Jaffa Gate.

A large opening in the wall between the Jaffa Gate and David's Citadel is the result of a visit to Jerusalem by Kaiser Wilhelm II of Germany in 1898. Among other reasons, the Kaiser journeyed to Jerusalem to dedicate his new Lutheran Church of the Redeemer located near the Church of the Holy Sepulchre. The Kaiser, a man given to pompous displays, wanted to enter the city on horseback, riding in a triumphal procession. The Arabs had strong objections to the Kaiser's plans because they viewed the entrance by a Christian on horseback as a symbol of conquest. Thus, the ruling Turks were faced with a perplexing dilemma– they were desirous of an alliance with the Kaiser, and the Kaiser was desirous of a parade. But the Turks also wanted to maintain peace with the local Arabs. Finally, someone suggested an acceptable compromise - tear down a portion of the wall in order that the Kaiser might ride his horse through the special opening instead of the gate. The Arabs kept their tradition, the Turks made their alliance with the Kaiser, the Kaiser had his parade, and the wall of Jerusalem got a huge hole in its side.

Because of the proximity of the Jaffa Gate to western Jerusalem, the Arabs sealed it shut after the War of Independence in 1948. It was reopened in 1967 by the Israelis.

THE CITADEL OF JERUSALEM

One of the most impressive structures of the Old City's walls is a fortress known as the Citadel of Jerusalem or David's Tower. When Titus destroyed Jerusalem in 70 A.D., he left standing three large towers which had been erected to defend Herod's palace. Herod had named the towers Phasael, in honor of his brother; Hippicus, after a friend; and Mariamne, for his wife whom he later murdered. The original towers were eventually destroyed, but the Crusaders erected the present Citadel on the ruins of one of the towers and used it as a palace for their kings.

The present structure is essentially from the Crusader period, although the Citadel was restored and enlarged by the Mamelukes in the fourteenth century and by Suleiman in the sixteenth century. It was originally surrounded by a deep moat. The Citadel was also used by the Turks for their army headquarters when they occupied Palestine. Later it was utilized by the Jordanian army.

Some scholars maintain that, in all probability, Christ was condemned to die by Pilate in the western palace of Herod near the present Citadel. It does not seem likely that Pilate would have stayed in the older palace at the Fortress of Antonia when he could have occupied the far more luxurious palace of Herod the Great.

Today Israel has transformed the Citadel into a beautiful cultural center where various concerts and programs are offered.

ישראל

ISRAEL

The Temple Mount

A view of the Old City from the Mount of Olives, with West Jerusalem blending into the skyline.

The Temple Mount

The thirty-five acre section of the Old City known as the Temple Mount is held in deep reverence by Christians, Jews, and Moslems. Solomon's Temple once stood upon its summit, as did the Temple of Herod the Great. Both houses of worship have long ago disappeared, but the ground where they stood remains holy, especially to the Jews. In fact, it is so sacred that Jews are cautioned by some religious leaders against even going onto the Temple Mount itself, lest they desecrate the Holy of Holies or walk on top of the Ark of the Covenant which may be buried there. Some Orthodox Jews believe that the Messiah will come and rebuild the Temple (Isaiah 2:2–3). Others believe that the Temple should be rebuilt as soon as possible. The latter view seems to be gaining in popularity. (See section on prophecy).

Known in the Scriptures as Mount Moriah, the hill of the Temple was the setting for Abraham's intended sacrifice of his son Isaac (Genesis 22). King David purchased the hill from Araunah and erected an altar there to atone for his sin of numbering the people (2 Samuel 24:18–25). David wanted to build the Temple, and even gathered the materials, but God would not permit it because he was a man of war. The Temple constructed about 950 B.C. by David's son and successor, Solomon, was destroyed in 586 B.C. by Nebuchadnezzar. The second Temple, much smaller and less elaborate, was erected under the leadership of Zerubbabel in 516 B.C. following the Babylonian captivity (Ezra).

Herod the Great, appointed by Rome as king of Israel in 40 B.C., was unpopular with his subjects, though himself a Jew. In an attempt to win the favor of his subjects, Herod announced in 22 B.C. that he would rebuild the Temple with a splendor exceeding the Temple of Solomon. The construction of the new Temple began two years later and took forty-six years to complete. Regardless of this and many other impressive building projects, however, Herod was never able to attain the admiration or respect of his subjects.

Herod's Temple was the scene for numerous events in the life of Jesus Christ. According to Jewish custom, Jesus was "presented" at the Temple by His parents on the fortieth day after His birth (Luke 2:21-39). When Jesus was twelve years of age, He accompanied His parents to Jerusalem again for the Feast of the Passover. On the journey back to Nazareth, Mary and Joseph discovered that He was missing from the caravan. After three days of searching, they found Him in the Temple (Luke 2:41-52). Twice Jesus cleansed the Temple by driving out the money-changers (John 2:13–22 and Matthew 21:12-13). On Palm Sunday Jesus rode on the back of a donkey through the Golden Gate and into the Temple area. Throughout the week preceeding His death, He taught there (Mark 11, 12, 13).

A number of incidents at the Temple involving Peter, John, Stephen, and Paul are recorded in the Book of Acts. Peter and John were imprisoned for their persistent proclamation of the Gospel there. Stephen so angered a crowd of worshippers that he was taken out and stoned to death. Paul barely escaped with his life as he attempted to proclaim the new, controversial message of Jesus to the Temple crowds.

The Arabs refer to the Temple Mount as the Haram esh-Sharif (Noble Sanctuary). Their sacred traditions concerning this site date back to the time of Mohammed, whom they believe ascended into heaven from the hill riding his winged horse, El Burak.

Located on the Temple Mount today are two buildings especially sacred to the Moslems- the Dome of the Rock and the Al Aksa Mosque. Each Friday, their congregational day of prayer, thousands of Moslems gather on the Temple Mount for worship and prayer.

THE DOME OF THE ROCK

Surely one of the most beautiful buildings in the world, the Dome of the Rock stands majestically near the site of the ancient Jewish Temple. Octagonal in shape, the shrine is adorned with 45,000 ornamental tiles. Centuries ago its dome was overlaid with gold leaf, but today it keeps a golden appearance through a covering of an aluminum-bronze alloy from Italy. Graceful marble columns supporting the dome date to the fourth century A.D. It is believed that these columns might have been reclaimed from Hadrian's temple to Jupiter which once stood on the site and from a Byzantine church which was located on the Mount of Olives, but their origin is not certain. Sixteen stained glass windows adorn the walls, which are elaborately decorated in various oriental designs, as well as the interior of the dome itself.

The Dome of the Rock, 176 feet in diameter, is built over a huge stone where tradition claims Abraham prepared to offer Isaac as a sacrifice, and where Mohammed was allegedly carried into heaven on his winged horse. The rock, 29 feet long and 39 feet wide, is surrounded by a railing. It is also believed that this rock was the location for Jewish sacrifices on the Temple Mount, evidenced by an extensive drain network carved out to carry off the blood of sacrificed animals.

The present structure dates to 691. The original building, constructed by Caliph Omar in 638, was frequently called the Mosque of Omar. Some authorities maintain that Omar's shrine was erected near the site of the Al Aksa Mosque.

Omar's wooden shrine was replaced in 691 with a building resembling the present edifice. Caliph Abd Al Malek, seeking to make Jerusalem rival Mecca and Medina in religious significance, set out to build a shrine without equal. He covered the dome's exterior with gold leaf. Caliph Malek's Dome of the Rock was damaged by an earthquake in 1016. Subsequently, it was damaged several times by such calamities, but always restored. In 1115 the Crusaders, thinking that the Dome of the Rock was really the Temple of Solomon, converted the Arab shrine into a church and called it the "Temple of the Lord." A fire seriously damaged the shrine in 1448, and it was restored for the final time by Suleiman the Magnificent in 1552.

THE AL AKSA MOSQUE

At the extreme southern portion of the Temple Mount is the third most sacred place in the Moslem religion, the Al Aksa Mosque. The present edifice, built in the eleventh century, is 262 feet in length and

180 feet in width, offering adequate room for over 5,000 worshippers. Moslems gather at the Al Aksa Mosque each Friday to pray and worship. Being a shrine and not a mosque, the Dome of the Rock is used only for personal prayers and devotion.

The original mosque was constructed in the seventh century by Caliph Waleed. The Crusader Knights of the Templers used the mosque as a royal palace and later as a dormitory.

Extensive renovations have been made to the mosque in recent years. On August 21, 1969, a young Australian, believed to be deranged, set fire to the Al Aksa Mosque, causing extensive damage. He claimed that he acted on orders from God in order to prepare for the rebuilding of the Temple. A hand-carved pulpit dating to the time of Saladin was destroyed in the fire. In 1978 the Egyptians replaced the pulpit in honor of President Anwar Sadat's visit to Jerusalem. Sadat had worshipped at the mosque during his historic visit to Israel in 1977.

Visitors who desire to enter the Dome of the Rock or the Al Aksa Mosque are required to remove their shoes and pass through strict security. Photography is not permitted inside either structure.

SOLOMON'S STABLES

Beneath the southeastern corner of the Temple Mount is a large subterranean room known as Solomon's Stables. Eighty-eight pillars in twelve rows, each 200 feet in length, form the stables where horses were kept during the Crusader period. There is no connection with Solomon. Some of the outer walls are Herodian. This underground area was originally built to support the Temple platform above.

THE PINNACLE OF THE TEMPLE

The extreme southeastern corner of the Temple Mount wall is called the "pinnacle of the Temple." Jesus was tempted by Satan to jump off the pinnacle in order to prove that He was the Messiah (Luke 4:9). Tradition tells us that James, the brother of Jesus and the first bishop of Jerusalem, was thrown off this pinnacle to his death.

A Jewish man praying at the Western Wall.

THE WESTERN WALL (KOTEL)

From 1948 to 1967, Jews were forbidden access to their most sacred place of worship, the Kotel, in full violation of international agreements. Known also as the Western Wall or the Wailing Wall, this outermost enclosure of the Temple Mount is one of the few portions of Herod's original structure not destroyed in 70 A.D. For centuries Jews have gathered before this remnant wall to weep and pray over the Temple's destruction. Some Jews believe that God's shekinah *presence* has never departed from the Western Wall.

The Wailing Wall, a name applied to the Kotel by the Gentiles because of the anguished sounds which some Jews make while praying there, rises to a height of sixty feet. It extends seventy feet below the surface where huge stones date to the days of Herod the Great. Stones visible at ground level also date to the time of Herod. One of the Herodian stones found in the underground passage extending from the Kotel measures thirty-nine feet in length, almost ten feet in height and thirteen feet in width. The small stones at the upper portion of the wall date to the nineteenth century.

Various Jewish rituals are performed at the Western Wall, including Bar Mitzvahs. As in Orthodox synagogues, the women are separated from the men at the Wall by a screen. In recent years, the area in front of the Kotel has been renovated with beautiful Jerusalem stone, making it possible for thousands to gather at the Wall for prayer. Prior to 1967, Arab houses filled the area in front of the Western Wall, leaving only a narrow alley for any assembly. However, immediately after the Israelis captured the Old City in 1967, they moved the Arabs to other quarters and tore down the houses in order to make room for the vast crowds which were expected at the Western Wall in prayer and celebration.

Non-Jews are permitted to pray at the Western Wall, but all men are required to wear hats. Crammed into the crevices between the stones are thousands of small pieces of paper containing prayer petitions. It is a most heartwarming experience to pray at the Wall for the "peace of Jerusalem."

As for the foreigner who does not belong to your people Israel
but has come from a distant land because of your great name
and your mighty hand and your outstretched arm- when he

comes and prays toward this temple, then hear from heaven, your dwelling place, and do whatever the foreigner asks of you, so that all the peoples of the earth may know your name and fear you, as do your own people Israel, and may know that this house I have built bears your Name

(2 Chronicles 6:32–33).

EXCAVATIONS AT THE SOUTHERN PORTION OF THE TEMPLE MOUNT

Excavations underneath and around the Temple Mount have been taking place for years. On the western side, older excavations reveal Wilson's arch and Robinson's arch. Both arches were part of a bridge which provided access to the Temple Mount from the upper city.

More recent excavations below the Al Aksa Mosque unearthed ancient stairs leading to the Temple. This Herodian staircase led from a public square to the Hulda Gate which contained both entrances and exits to the Temple platform from the lower part of the city. Inside the Hulda Gate were long tunnels leading to and from the Temple area. A triple gate and a double gate were both known as the Hulda Gate. It is believed that the triple gate was used for entry and the double gate was used for exiting the Temple Mount. There is little doubt that Jesus and His disciples walked these stairs as they made their way to and from the Temple.

Three arches of the Hulda Gate are clearly visible to the right of the steps. The tunnel for the triple gate is gone, but the one for the double gate remains. The inner walls of the tunnel are original, as are the elaborately carved domes in the ceiling which date to the Herodian period. The domes, 16 feet in diameter, were painted in bright colors.

Jewish ritual baths known as miqva'ot also were unearthed near the Hulda Gates. These baths were for spiritual cleansing only. Similar miqva'ot were found at Masada. The baths contained steps leading down to a reservoir, as well as a separate set for exiting. Complete immersion was involved in these Jewish ritual baths. There are some scholars who believe that they may have been used for early Christian baptisms, such as those described in Acts 2.

ישראל

ISRAEL

The Valleys
Around Jerusalem

The Valleys Around Jerusalem

Three deep valleys which once nearly encircled the Old City have great significance not only to Jerusalem's topography but also to the city's history. The valleys are mentioned often in Scripture, especially the Old Testament. Essentially the three valleys provided an added measure of defense, making the walls more difficult to approach by an enemy. Only the northside of the city was without a valley beneath its walls. Instead, the northern wall was often protected by numerous defense towers and a deep moat.

THE KIDRON VALLEY, the most historic and sacred of the three valleys, originates at the base of Mount Scopus and extends southward to the Dead Sea. At its extreme northern portion, the Kidron measures about 2600 feet above sea level, dropping to 2000 feet above sea level where it joins the Valley of Hinnom in the south. Its northern portion was known in the Old Testament as the Valley of Jehoshaphat.

The Valley of Jehoshaphat, which literally means "God's valley of judgment," has long been associated by Jews, Christians and Moslems as the scene of Judgment Day. Desiring to be among the first resurrected, members of all three religions used the area for their burial grounds (Joel 3:1-2).

Flowing through the center of the Kidron Valley is a small brook called by the same name. The brook is mentioned in the Bible in association with David's flight from his rebellious son, Absalom (2 Samuel 15:23). It is really a dry wadi much of the year, containing water only during the rainy season.

The Gospel of John tells of Jesus crossing the Kidron Valley with His disciples as they made their way from the Upper Room to the Garden of Gethsemane on the night of His betrayal and arrest (18:1).

THE VALLEY OF HINNOM, known in ancient times as Topheth or Gehenna, extends from the base of the present-day Mount Zion to the Kidron Valley. Its only positive reference in Scripture identifies it as a boundary between the tribes of Judah and Benjamin (Joshua 15:8 and 18:16). Other references identify Hinnom as a place of evil and wickedness. Idol worship and child sacrifice, even by kings of Israel, took place in Hinnom (2 Chronicles 28:3 and 33:6). As punishment for these abominations, God's hand of judgment fell upon Judah (Jeremiah 7:30-34).

A portion of Hinnom was used as the city dump. Fires which continuously burned there to consume the rubbish became illustrative of a burning hell. The Greek New Testament word "Gehenna" was used in place of the Hebrew word "Hinnom." It is interesting to note the juxtaposition of the Valley of Hinnom (hell) and the Valley of Jehoshaphat (judgment).

Within the Valley of Hinnom, near its junction with the Kidron, is the scene of another great tragedy. The area is known as Akeldama (Field of Blood), the place where Judas took his own life after betraying Jesus for thirty pieces of silver (Acts 1:19).

THE TYROPEON VALLEY, which begins at the Damascus Gate and descends to the juncture of Hinnom and Kidron just above the Pool of Siloam, actually cuts the city into two parts. Once a deep valley, it is now filled with the debris of many centuries, making it most difficult to locate within the Old City itself. However, from outside the wall to the Pool of Siloam, its descent is still very steep.

In the days of Herod, the Tyropeon Valley divided the upper and the lower portions of the city. A high bridge, supported by several arches, spanned the valley and provided residents of the upper city a ready access to the Temple Mount. Two of those ancient arches may still be seen at the Temple Mount. The one which supported the stairs is known as Robinson Arch, and the other which supported the bridge is called the Wilson Arch, named for the archeologists who discovered them.

ישראל

ISRAEL

In And Around
The Old City

In And Around The Old City

SAINT ANNE'S CHURCH

North of the Temple enclosure and near Lion's Gate is an outstanding Crusader edifice, the Church of Saint Anne. Tradition maintains that the church is built over the home of Joachim and Anne, parents of the Virgin Mary, and that Mary was born there.

In 1192 Saladin converted the church into a Moslem school for religious studies. Still visible is an Arab inscription that he placed over the door. The church remained in Arab hands until 1856 when the Turks gave it to the French. It is maintained today by the French White Fathers. Heavily damaged in the Six Day War of 1967, the church has undergone major renovation.

THE POOL OF BETHESDA

Excavations adjacent to Saint Anne's Church, begun in 1876, revealed the ancient site of the Pool of Bethesda as recorded in the New Testament. Uncovered are the ruins of a Byzantine church, a Crusader church, and portions of two ancient pools. At the Pool of Bethesda, Jesus healed a man who had been crippled for thirty-eight years (John 5:1-9).

THE FORTRESS OF ANTONIA

Named in honor of Mark Antony and built at the northwest corner of the Temple Mount, the Fortress of Antonia was one of Herod's great building projects, serving both as his palace and as barracks for a garrison of Roman soldiers. Its location made it a good observation post for the potentially troublesome Temple area and a strong defense for the city's vulnerable northern side. Herod used the Fortress of Antonia for his residence until his own elaborate palace on the western side of the city was completed. Fearing the Jews, the king constructed a secret passage for himself from the fortress to the Temple area. All that exists of the fortress today is a portion of the foundation. A staircase, supposedly from Antonia and known as the Scala Sancta, was removed and taken to Rome centuries ago where it may be seen today in the ancient papal church, Saint John's Lateran. Catholic tradition maintains that Christ walked these stairs on His way to the Cross. Martin Luther was one of many pilgrims to climb the stairs on his knees when he visited Rome as a young priest.

Some scholars assert that Pilate was staying at the Fortress of Antonia when he sentenced Jesus to die. It was common for Roman procurators to leave Caesarea and reside in Jerusalem during special Jewish holy days, in order to help maintain a peace which was always fragile at best. The Scriptures connect the palace and the praetorium (Mark 15:16), but it is uncertain if the praetorium was at the Fortress of Antonia or at the western palace.

Within the Fortress of Antonia was a courtyard called the "pavement" (lithostrotos in Greek, gabbatha in Hebrew) where Jesus Christ was condemned to die by Pontius Pilate (John 19: 13). Near the "pavement" is the Ecce Homo Arch, visible in the lower portions of the Sisters of Sion Convent. The arch, dating to the time of Hadrian, supposedly marks the place where Jesus, scourged and crowned with thorns, was presented to the crowds as Pilate declared, "Behold the Man!" (Ecce Homo).

One may view inside the Convent portions of pavement dating from the time of Hadrian. The ancient streets were several feet lower than the streets are today. On some of the Hadrian pavement stones are markings of a Roman game known as *Basilinda* (the King). The game apparently was played by Roman soldiers to pass the time and to abuse the prisoners. It was a cruel game involving ridicule, beatings and torture. The game could explain the manner in which Christ was abused prior to His crucifixion.

In 66 A.D. the Fortress of Antonia was captured by the Jews during their revolt against Rome. They held it until 70 A.D. when it was recaptured by Titus following a long, fierce and bloody struggle. The Romans used the Fortress of Antonia to lay siege to the Temple area, subsequently destroying both, together with the entire city of Jerusalem.

THE VIA DOLOROSA

Roman and Orthodox Catholics, observing traditions dating to Crusader times, have marked out what they believe to be the route of Jesus from Pilate's residence to His crucifixion on Golgotha. They call it the Via Dolorosa (the Way of Sorrow). There are fourteen "stations of the cross" along the route. Each station identifies a place where tradition contends that a specific event took place in Jesus' journey to the cross. These stations have become a part of Catholic worship and devotion. Each Friday in Jerusalem's Old City, Christians trace the steps of Christ from Pilate's judgment hall at Antonia to the hill of Calvary inside the Church of the Holy Sepulchre. The processions on Good Friday usually involve thousands of pilgrims. Two stations of the cross are located in the area of the Praetorium, seven are located on the street, and the remaining five are found inside the Church of the Holy Sepulchre.

STATION I   - Fortress of Antonia. (An Arab school marks the place where Christ was sentenced to die and from where His journey to the cross began.)

STATION II   - Chapel of the Flagellation and the Chapel of Scourging. (Christ was beaten and forced to take up His cross.)

STATION III   - Polish Catholic Church/museum. (Christ fell for the first time).

STATION IV   - Franciscan Church. (Christ met His mother.)

STATION V   - (Christ fell for the second time. Simon of Cyrene compelled to carry His cross.)

STATION VI   - House of Veronica. (Veronica wiped the brow of Jesus. The imprint of His face remained on the cloth.)

STATION VII   - (Location of the Gate of Judgment where

Good Friday procession on the Via Dolorosa.

Christ went out of the city. The order for
His execution may have been posted on
the gate.)

STATION VIII - Greek Monastery. (Christ encountered
the women of Jerusalem and told them
not to weep for Him but for themselves
and their children.)

STATION IX - Entrance to Coptic Church. (Christ fell
for the third time.)

STATION X - Church of the Holy Sepulchre. (Jesus was
stripped of His garments and the soldiers
cast lots for them.)

STATION XI - Church of the Holy Sepulchre. (Christ
was nailed to the cross.)

STATION XII - Church of the Holy Sepulchre. (Location
of the crucifixion.)

STATION XIII - Church of the Holy Sepulchre. (Place
where Christ's body was prepared for
burial.)

STATION XIV - Church of the Holy Sepulchre. (At the
tomb where Christ was buried.)

THE CHURCH OF THE HOLY SEPULCHRE

The Via Dolorosa (The Way of Sorrow) ends at the Church of the
Holy Sepulchre, one of the world's oldest and most revered
churches. According to Catholic tradition, the church is built over
the hill of Calvary and the tomb where Christ was buried.

In 325 Constantine sent his mother, Helena, to the Holy Land to
locate the various meaningful places from the life of Christ. Aided
in her efforts by Eusebius, Bishop of Caesarea, and Marcarius,
Bishop of Jerusalem, the search was undertaken. Constantine further
directed that the pagan temples erected by Hadrian in the second century be torn down. In the process of razing the temple of Jupiter, the
hill of Calvary and the tomb of Jesus were discovered. Many scholars believe that Hadrian built his temples on the Christian holy sites
in order to stamp out every vestige of Christianity. The irony is that

Hadrian's temples may have actually helped to identity the locations of important events in the life of Christ.

Other scholars have argued that the Church of the Holy Sepulchre could not have been the location of the crucifixion because it is situated inside the first-century walls of Jerusalem. While recent excavations prove that the site on which the Church of the Holy Sepulchre is located was definitely outside a wall, some scholars believe it was an inner-defense wall and not part of the outer wall.

Dedicated in 335, the original church structure was destroyed in 614; a second structure was destroyed in 1010. The Crusaders erected a church building on the site in 1149, similar in design to the present church. This third church was extensively damaged by fire in 1808. Portions of the present building still date to Crusader times. In recent years the church has been undergoing a sorely needed renovation.

The Church of the Holy Sepulchre is controlled today by the Greek Orthodox, Latins, Armenians, Coptics and Syrians. Bitter quarrels have erupted through the years among these various groups concerning rights to the church. The keys of the church are in the hands of two Moslem families, a tradition which extends from the time of Saladin.

Just inside the church's main entrance are stairs leading to the top of Calvary's hill. At that level are located three stations of the cross as well as various works of art. A Greek Orthodox altar stands over the place where Christ was crucified. Visitors may reach down through the floor to touch the hill itself. According to Catholic tradition, Adam is buried directly beneath the hill of Calvary. This tradition further maintains that, at the time of Christ's crucifixion, the hill split open and Jesus' blood fell on Adam's remains.

Catholic tradition also teaches that Christ's body was prepared for burial on a large stone located just inside the main entrance of the church. The tomb itself is located in the very center of the church in a chapel beneath the dome. The first section is called the Angels' Chapel, marking the place where the angels rolled back the stone which sealed the tomb. The next section is located over the tomb itself. The Church is a great disappointment for many people. It is dark and dingy. The noise and commotion lend little to reverence or worship. One tends to feel as Mary Magdalene on that first Easter morning when she said, "They have taken away my Lord, and I do not know where they have laid him." Commenting on his trip to Jerusalem, Mark Twain stated, "One finds it difficult to realize that Christ was not crucified in a Catholic church." Even the very liberal Harry Emerson Fosdick urged pilgrims to go to Gordon's Calvary to gain an appreciation for the meaning of Christ's death and resurrection.

GORDON'S CALVARY

The highlight of a pilgrimage to the Holy Land for most evangelical Christians is a visit to the Garden Tomb and Gordon's Calvary. Located a short distance north of the Damascus Gate, the site is believed by many to be the placed where Christ was crucified, buried and, most importantly, resurrected. No church or shrine covers this place. Its natural beauty is carefully maintained by the Garden Tomb Association, a British organization which purchased the three-acre tract in 1894. The site was discovered in 1885 by a British military officer, Charles G. Gordon, as he walked the wall of the Old City. Looking to the north, not far from the Damascus Gate, Gordon pondered a hillside which seemed to fit the biblical description of the place where Jesus was crucified. Later, as Gordon and others studied the site, they observed the distinctive markings of a skull-like formation on the side of the hill. Gordon was convinced that a verse in Leviticus was of great importance in a consideration of the true location of Jesus' death. He later wrote:

> This morning after my arrival at Jerusalem I went to the Skull Hill, and felt convinced that it must be north of the Altar. Leviticus 1:11 says that the victims are to be slain on the side of the Altar north-wards (literally to be slain slantwise or askew on the north of the Altar); if a particular direction was given by God about where the types were to be slain, it is a sure deduction that the prototype would be slain in some position as the Altar; this the Skull Hill fulfills. . . . The Latin Holy Sepulchre is west of the Altar, and therefore, unless types are wrong, it should never have been taken as the site.

Having questioned the credibility of the Church of the Holy Sepulchre as the location of Christ's death and burial, Gordon began to

Skull-shaped hill at Gordon's Calvary.

make further inquiries. Convinced that the rocky hill with the features of a skull might well be the location of Jesus' crucifixion and burial, he urged a group in England to purchase the property, which they did.

A rocky hill even with the shape of a skull was not adequate proof of the site, however. If this was the place of Jesus' crucifixion, there had to be a tomb nearby. Earlier excavations had, in fact, unearthed a tomb carved out of solid rock and dating to the first century. More than that, they later discovered a huge first-century cistern, indisputable evidence that the site had once been a garden. John describes the scene of Calvary and the garden in his gospel:

> At the place where Jesus was crucified, there was a garden, and in the garden a new tomb, in which no one had ever been laid. Because it was the Jewish day of Preparation and since the tomb was nearby, they laid Jesus there
>
> *(John 19: 41–42).*

Other factors also point to this site. The area was once a quarry, making it a natural place for executions, especially stonings. There is evidence to suggest that Stephen might have been stoned to death here. That theory is supported, in part, by the discovery of ancient ruins from a church in the area, named in honor of the first Christian martyr. Furthermore, it is known that in Roman times this area had been a busy thoroughfare and that the Romans usually carried out their crucifixions in well-traveled areas.

In the same general vicinity and adjacent to the Garden Tomb are several tombs dating as far back as the first-Temple period. Beneath a Dominican monastery next door to the Garden Tomb is an outstanding burial cave also dating to the first-Temple period. Some scholars maintain that the Garden Tomb is from the first-Temple era. They point out that the tomb's two side by side chambers were typical of tombs constructed in that period. At the time of Jesus many of the tombs also had two chambers, but the second chamber was usually behind the first. However, it is known that tombs with the side by side chambers also were constructed at the time of Christ. The Gospel accounts clearly report that the tomb in which Jesus was buried was new and never used. Further, the gospels state that one could look into the tomb from the entrance and see the burial chamber. Such would not have been possible if the more common construction had been used in the tomb of Joseph of Arimathea.

Two other striking pieces of evidence from Scripture also lend credence to this site as the place of Christ's death, burial, and resurrection. An ancient tradition holds that Jeremiah was imprisoned in a nearby cave when he wrote his Lamentations. This cave is clearly visible from the hill of Calvary. In a deeply moving portion of prophecy which pictures Christ's crucifixion, Jeremiah asks, "Is it nothing to you who pass by?" Is it not possible that the Lord might have inspired Jeremiah to pen those words on the very location where the event would one day occur?

The second Scripture passage, more specific and undeniably related to Jesus' death and resurrection, is found in Genesis 22. The entire chapter details Abraham's obedient response to God's command that he offer his only son, Isaac, on Mount Moriah. The hill of Gordon's Calvary is at the northernmost portion of the mount. The Temple stood at the southern end. The entire twenty-second chapter of Genesis presents Isaac as a type of Christ and prophetically looks forward to the event of Christ's death. There are numerous parallels between the actions of Abraham and Isaac and those of God, the Father, and Jesus, the Son. Throughout the account, Abraham is guided by God to "the place" where he is to make the sacrifice on Mount Moriah. In every one of the gospel accounts, the writers refer to Calvary as "the place." On the opposite end of Mount Moriah stood the Temple where sacrifices for sin were offered. Every animal slain on the Temple's altar pointed forward to "the Lamb of God who takes away the sin of the world" (John 1:29). How prophetic that Abraham told his son, Isaac, that "God Himself shall provide the Lamb." And how fitting that on the same mountain Jesus would offer His own body and blood as the eternal, once for all atonement for man's sins.

William Steuart McBirnie's book *The Search for the Tomb of Jesus* presents an outstanding case for the site of Gordon's Calvary and the Garden Tomb as the authentic location of these events in the life of Jesus.

The Garden Tomb Association provides guides who carefully explain the spiritual meaning of Calvary and the empty tomb to visitors and pilgrims. Little effort is made by these guides to convince people

The Garden Tomb where many believe Jesus was buried and resurrected.

as to the authenticity of the location, but much effort is made to witness to the fact that Jesus Christ, once crucified, is alive today and that He is reaching out to bring life abundantly to all who will receive Him.

In front of the empty tomb and throughout the garden, benches are provided so that Christians may sit to worship and pray. Many of their services include Holy Communion. Over 100,000 Christians visit the Garden Tomb each year. Pilgrims are permitted to enter the tomb to "behold the place where He lay." Standing quietly in the midst of the garden with its many flower-lined paths one may hear songs of praise in various languages as Christians from all over the world worship the Lord of Life.

While many hold tenaciously to the Church of the Holy Sepulchre or Gordon's Calvary as the true site of the crucifixion and the burial place of Christ, the truth of Christ's victory over death is vastly more important than its location. We do well to remember that Jesus' bones are not interred in any tomb. He lives! Were it possible for us to correctly discover all the sacred places in the life of Christ and dedicate the rest of our lives to worshipping before them, our salvation would not be secured. "Yet to all who receive him, to those who believe in his name, he gave the right to become children of God" (John 1:12). "Because you have seen me, you have believed; blessed are those who have not seen and yet have believed" (John 20:29).

THE TOMBS OF THE KINGS

A short distance to the north of the Damascus Gate and near St. George Street are the ancient Tombs of the Kings, excavated in 1863. Many elaborate sarcophagi were found at that time, some of which are now housed in the Louvre in Paris. Dating to the first century they are among the finest tombs ever unearthed in Israel. Queen Helena of Mesopotamia and her family were buried here (not to be confused with Helena, mother of Constantine). Within the tomb complex is a court measuring 91 by 82 feet. The vestibule is 34 feet wide.

THE ROCKEFELLER MUSEUM

The Rockefeller Museum, built in 1928 at a cost of $2,000,000 with funds from John D. Rockefeller, contains an outstanding collection of antiquities from various archaeological excavations made principally between 1920 and 1948. Located adjacent to the northeastern corner of the Old City, the museum is open to visitors seven days a week.

THE CITY OF DAVID

Ancient Jebusite-Jerusalem became known as the City of David following its capture by Israel's second monarch. Accounts of its conquest are given in 2 Samuel 5:6-9 and 1 Chronicles 11:4-7. David's City was very small in comparison with Jerusalem at the time of Christ and especially with Jerusalem of today. It is likely that the Jebusites located the city at the base of Mount Moriah because of the Gihon Spring.

The ancient city has undergone extensive excavations in the last thirty years. Sidewalks and steps were constructed throughout the northernmost excavations in order that visitors may view the many exciting discoveries which uncovered centuries of Jerusalem's history. A Jebusite wall built around 1800 B.C. may be viewed at this archaeological site, as well as an Israelite wall constructed about 750 B.C. and a portion of Nehemiah's wall dating to 445 B.C. The ruins of a tower from the time of the Maccabees may also be seen. The charred ruins of an Israelite home destroyed at the time of Jerusalem's fall in 586 B.C. are among the most interesting discoveries at the site. A number of ancient tombs have been excavated in the lower portion of the city. Many scholars believe that this is the true location of David's tomb which, as yet, has not been discovered.

THE GIHON SPRING AND THE POOL OF SILOAM

The Gihon Spring at the western side of the Kedron Valley was the primary source of water for the ancient city of Jerusalem. Known also as the Virgin's Fountain it is connected to the Pool of Siloam by a tunnel which is 1748 feet long. When Sennacherib threatened to invade Judah in 70l, King Hezekiah recognized that Jerusalem's water supply outside the walls made the city extremely vulnerable to any aggressor. Thus, he ordered the construction of a tunnel for the purpose of bringing the waters of the Gihon inside the city's walls (2 Chronicles 32:30 and 2 Kings 20:20). Because of the emergency nature of the project, two crews set to work, one from the spring and the other from Siloam. They carved the tunnel out of solid rock, an enormous task in that day, and met exactly at the designated point, a remarkable engineering accomplishment. The two pools at Siloam, inside the city's walls, served as reservoirs for Jerusalem's inhabitants.

Two boys playing at the Pool of Siloam in 1880 accidently found an ancient inscription written on stone and dating to 700 B.C. It reads as follows:

> The boring through is completed. And this is the story of the boring through: while yet they plied the drill each toward his fellow, and while there was heard the voice of one calling unto another, for there was a crevice in the rock on the right hand. And on the day of the boring through, the stone-cutters struck, each to meet his fellow, drill upon drill; and the water flowed from the source to the pool for a thousand and two hundred cubits, and a hundred cubits was the height of the rock above the heads of the stone-cutters.

The present reservoir at Siloam is fifty-two feet in length and sixteen feet in width. One is reminded of the time when Jesus instructed a blind man at the Temple to wash his eyes in the Pool of Siloam. "So he went and washed and came back seeing" (John 9:1-34).

Jebusite-Jerusalem's location was largely due to the Gihon Spring. In a less sophisticated manner, the Jebusites had constructed a shaft from inside Jerusalem to the Gihon. King David was able to take the city from the Jebusites by sending his men through the shaft and into the city (2 Samuel 5:8). David had Solomon crowned king at Gihon as Absalom was conducting his rebellion (1 Kings l).

Today one may walk the length of the tunnel, but it is an experience for only the most energetic pilgrims.

KING SOLOMON'S QUARRIES

In 1854 a man walking his dog accidentally discovered the ancient quarries of Solomon where it is believed stones for the Temple were cut and dressed (I Kings 6:7). The sound of the hammer was not permitted at the Temple site itself. The quarries extend under a section of the northern part of the city and may be entered a short distance from the Damascus Gate.

MOUNT ZION

The name Mount Zion is mentioned often in Scriptures and refers to the Temple Mount, the entire city of Jerusalem or to Israel. Today the name also identifies an area of Jerusalem more properly called the Western Hill.

At the time of Jesus, the Western Hill was within the city walls, but today it is situated a short distance outside the walls. Mount Zion or the Western Hill is sacred to the Jews because of their tradition that King David was buried there. The Roman Catholics revere the site as the place where Mary the mother of Jesus fell eternally asleep. Many Christians recognize Mount Zion as the location of the Upper Room where Christ shared the "Last Supper" with His disciples and where the Holy Spirit was poured out on the day of Pentecost. It is known that several ancient churches were built on this hill as Christians sought to elevate its importance. In fact, some believe that the first Christian church building was erected on the Western Hill. It was probably those early Christians who renamed it Mount Zion.

During the 1948 War of Independence, Israel was unable to capture any part of the Old City, but was successful in maintaining control of Mount Zion.

THE UPPER ROOM

For evangelical Christians the most significant site on Mount Zion is the Upper Room or Coneneculum (Latin for "dining room"). It obviously is not the original Upper Room, but ancient Christian tradition places the room of the Last Supper at this location. The fourteenth-century structure where the present Upper Room is located was built on the foundations of a fourth-century church known as Holy Zion, "the mother of all churches," destroyed in 614. The building housing the Upper Room was converted into a Moslem shrine in 1524, and Christians were barred from going there. Israel opened the Upper Room to everyone in 1948.

To enter the Upper Room, one must first climb a set of recently constructed stone stairs. The original steps were nearly worn away through centuries of use. A Moslem prayer-niche is visible on a wall of the Upper Room, as well as a Crusader coat of arms which was recently discovered near the exit.

Jesus shared the Passover with His disciples in the Upper Room the night before His crucifixion. In an act of deep humility following the meal, Jesus washed their feet and offered to them the bread and wine of the new covenant. Ten days after Jesus' ascension, the Holy Spirit was poured out upon 120 people who were gathered in the Upper Room (Acts 2).

THE TOMB OF KING DAVID

There is little to authenticate the site of David's Tomb, but Jews regard its importance second only to the Western Wall. While the Western Wall symbolizes Israel's religious hopes, the Tomb of David symbolizes their national hopes. What is called the Tomb of David today was discovered near the traditional Upper Room during the Crusader period. Since its discovery, Jews have gathered before the tomb for prayer. However, most scholars believe that David's tomb is somewhere in the area south of the Temple Mount. Crowns of the Torah from European synagogues were placed above the tomb until 1978. After several of the crowns were stolen, most were taken to the Israel National Museum for safekeeping.

THE DORMITION CHURCH AND MONASTERY

Dominating the skyline of Mount Zion is the impressive Benedictine Abbey of the Dormition with its beautiful church. Built by Kaiser Wilhelm II who wanted Germany well represented at the sacred places of the Holy Land, the church was consecrated in 1910. The Church of the Dormition is built over the place where Roman Catholic tradition maintains Mary fell eternally asleep before being assumed into heaven. In the crypt below the sanctuary a stone sculpture depicts Mary lying on her deathbed. Above it is a brightly decorated cupola which depicts Jesus calling His blessed mother to heaven. Small chapels around the stone image of Mary were donated by Catholics from various nations.

SAINT PETER IN GALLICANTU

On the edge of the Western Hill overlooking the Pool of Siloam stands a Roman Catholic church erected over the ruins of the house of Caiaphas, the high priest. An ancient Byzantine church once stood on the same ruins, but it was destroyed in 1109. The present Church, built in 1931 by the Assumptionist Fathers, is known as the Church of Saint Peter in Gallicantu (Latin for "cockcrow").

After Jesus was arrested in the Garden of Gethsemane, He was first taken to the house of Caiaphas (Mark 14:53-66). While Jesus was being questioned and abused by His captors, Peter stood warming himself by the fire in the courtyard. There, fulfilling the prophecy of Jesus, Peter denied the Lord three times before the crowing of the cock (Mark 14:66-72).

The interior of the church is adorned with mosaics which depict various scenes of Christ's sufferings. From the outer balcony of the church, one may view a portion of the Kidron Valley and the Mount of Olives. Directly below the balcony are the ruins of olive presses, a bath house and several caves. Stone steps which date to the first century are also visible leading to the Valley of the Cheesemakers below. It is likely that Christ was led up these steps following His arrest in the Garden of Gethsemane.

The ruins of the high priest's prison are located in the lowest level of the church. It is believed that Jesus was confined there overnight. Pillars with holes carved out reveal how prisoners were tied and beaten. Chiseled out of the floor near the pillars are other holes which held a water and vinegar solution which was used to revive prisoners who fainted from whippings. There is a large pit in another section of the prison, similar to the pit described in Jeremiah 37 and 38, where prisoners were lowered by ropes through an overhead opening. Psalm 88 prophetically describes Jesus alone in the pit prior to His crucifixion. Ancient crosses painted on the walls indicate that Christians revered this site centuries ago.

O Lord, the God who saves me,
day and night I cry out before you.
May my prayer come before you;
turn your ear to my cry.
For my soul is full of trouble
and my life draws near the grave.
I am counted among those who go down to the pit;
I am like a man without strength.
I am set apart with the dead, like the slain
who lie in the grave, whom you remember no more,
who are cut off from your care.
You have put me in the lowest pit,
in the darkest depths.
Your wrath lies heavily upon me;
you have overwhelmed me with all your waves.
You have taken from me my closest friends
and have made me repulsive to them.
I am confined and cannot escape;
my eyes are dim with grief.
You have taken my companions and loved ones
from me; the darkness is my closest friend.

Psalm 88:1-9,18.

THE MOUNT OF OLIVES

"As the mountains surround Jerusalem, so the Lord surrounds his people, both now and forevermore"

(Psalm 125:2).

Mentioned frequently in Scripture, the Mount of Olives rises to a height of 2674 feet above sea level, dominating the skyline of Jerusalem's eastern side. One experiences a breathtaking panoramic view of Jerusalem from its two-mile-long summit. Looking to the east, it is possible to see across the Judean desert to the Dead Sea and beyond to the Mountains of Moab. On the slopes of the Mount of Olives are thousands of tombstones which mark the graves of Christians, Jews and Moslems who had hoped to be among the first summoned at the resurrection.

Jesus often walked with His disciples on the Mount of Olives and taught them many things there regarding the Kingdom of God. It was on Mount Olivet that Jesus gave a most extensive message about end times. On Olivet's slopes He pronounced God's impending judgment upon Jerusalem (Matthew 24). Interestingly, Titus gathered his forces on the Mount of Olives and on Mount Scopus before besieging and destroying the city in 70 A.D.

The little village of Bethany is located on the eastern summit of the Mount of Olives. Jesus frequently visited Lazarus, Mary and Martha in their Bethany home. On one memorable visit, He raised Lazarus from the dead (John 11). A church designed by the Italian architect Barlucci commemorates this event. The Church of Lazarus resembles a tomb, with its only light coming from the ceiling. Nearby is a first-century tomb which tradition considers to be the tomb of Lazarus.

From Bethphage, another Olivet village, Jesus sent His disciples to borrow a donkey on which He rode down Olivet's slopes and through Jerusalem's Golden Gate. The Palm Sunday road today, set apart by a wall on each side, concludes at the base of Olivet near the Garden of Gethsemane. Halfway down the Palm Sunday road stands the Teardrop Church (Dominus Flevet), the traditional site where Jesus wept over Jerusalem. "Would that even today you knew the things that make for peace" (Luke 19:28–47). Farther down the road and just above the Garden of Gethsemane is the beautiful Russian Orthodox Church of Saint Mary Magdalene with its golden onion-shaped domes.

Forty days after the resurrection Jesus walked with His disciples to the summit of the Mount of Olives where He commissioned them to take the Gospel to the whole world. As they looked on, He was lifted into the clouds and out of their sight. Two angels assured the disciples that Jesus would come again in the same manner as they had seen Him go (Acts 1:6-11 and Zechariah 14:4).

An octagonal-shaped building known as the Chapel of the Ascension stands on the summit of the Mount of Olives, marking the traditional place of the ascension. The original structure, built in the fourth century, reportedly had no roof. The present chapel was

The Church of All Nations at the Garden of Gethsemane.

rebuilt by the Crusaders; the walls which enclose the structure were built later by the Moslems. Inside, visitors are shown the very "footprint of Jesus," a most incredible deception. The chapel is controlled today by the Moslems. Nearby is the Russian Orthodox Church and Tower of the Ascension. Obviously, the exact location of the ascension is not known; the Scriptures state only that it was on the Mount of Olives and near Bethany (Luke 24:50–51).

On the summit of the Mount of Olives also stands the Pater Noster Church (Church of the Lord's Prayer), built on the ruins of a fourth-century church and a Crusader church. Tradition maintains that Jesus taught the Lord's Prayer here. The present church was erected in 1868, and the Lord's Prayer is written in fifty-two languages on its exterior walls.

One of the most imposing structures on the Mount of Olives is the Augusta Victoria Hospital, built originally by Kaiser Wilhelm II as a hospice for returning missionaries and German pilgrims. However, the elaborate building was little used for that purpose, and since World War I it has been utilized as a hospital. Today the hospital is operated by the Lutheran World Federation as a service to the Arab people on the West Bank. The Augusta Victoria Hospital complex contains a beautiful church with a magnificent tower, a landmark of Jerusalem's eastern skyline. The church and hospital were heavily damaged in the wars of 1948 and 1967. On the extreme eastern side of the hospital grounds is a unique outdoor worship area which offers a commanding view of the Judean desert. The view is especially beautiful in late afternoon when the sun paints the desert in a hundred shades of brown.

THE GARDEN OF GETHSEMANE

The Garden of Gethsemane, one of Scripture's most hallowed scenes, is located at the base of the Mount of Olives, directly below the Eastern Gate. It is likely that Jesus chose this beautiful place for prayer many times, either alone or with His disciples. We know for a fact that He chose this secluded garden on the night of His arrest and betrayal. Judas also knew the place well and easily led the temple guard to the scene of Christ's lonely agony. While Jesus prayed, His disciples slept.

Priest at prayer in the Garden of Gethsemane.

Eight olive trees with root systems at least 1000 years old grace the well-kept Garden today. The Garden and the Church of All Nations nearby are under the care of the Franciscans. The Church of All Nations, built in 1927 at a cost of two million dollars, was also designed by Barlucci. Constructed over the ruins of fourth-century and Crusader churches, the present structure incorporates portions of an ancient church floor from the fourth century. A large rock in front of the church marks the place where Catholic tradition claims that Jesus agonized in prayer. A beautiful mosaic of the Lord praying in Gethsemane adorns the wall above the main altar. A series of domes constructed through the contributions of individuals from various nations of the world cover the sanctuary. Windows made of dark stained glass help to create an effect of perpetual night and a somber mood.

To know the precise place within the Garden where Christ prayed is impossible. But it is sufficient to know that what He did here was for us and for our salvation.

> For me it was in the Garden
> that He prayed "not my will but thine."
> He had no tears for His own grief,
> but shed drops of blood for mine.
> How marvelous, how wonderful,
> and my song shall ever be;
> How marvelous, how wonderful
> is my Savior's love for me.
>
> *Charles H. Gabriel*

ישראל

ISRAEL

In And Around
West Jerusalem

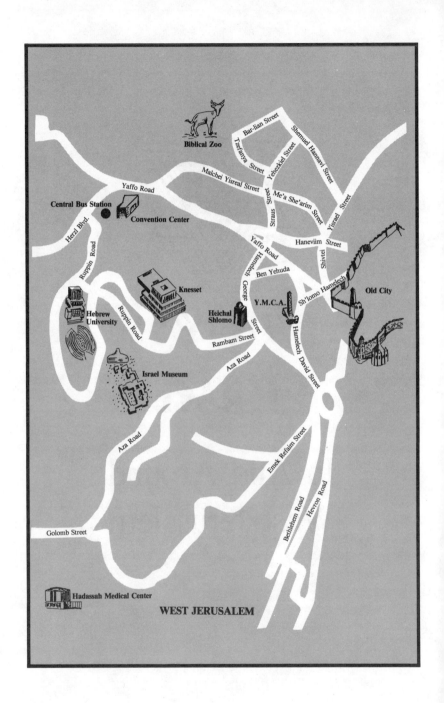

Biblical Zoo

Bar-lian Street

Shemuel Hannavi Street

Tzefanya Street

Yehezkiel Street

Malchei Yisreal Street

Street

Me'a She'arim Street

Yisrael Street

Yaffo Road

Central Bus Station

Convention Center

Straus

Yaffo Road

Haneviim Street

Shivtei

Herzl Blvd.

Hamelech

Ben Yehuda

Ruppin Road

Knesset

George

Old City

Sh'lomo Hamelech

Hebrew
University

Ruppin Road

Heichal
Shlomo

Y.M.C.A.

Street

Rambam Street

Hamelech David Street

Israel Museum

Aza Road

Aza Road

Emek Refaim Street

Bethlehem Road

Hevron Road

Golomb Street

Hadassah Medical Center

WEST JERUSALEM

In And Around West Jerusalem

The crown jewel of Israel is her national capital, Jerusalem. Over the protests of the United Nations, Israel declared Jerusalem as her capital in 1949. Under the original United Nations' partition plan, Jerusalem was to become an international city, in spite of the fact that its population had been predominantly Jewish for over a hundred years. The Jews were reluctantly willing to accept the internationalization of Jerusalem, if it meant the establishment of their long-desired nation, but the Arabs were not so inclined. Then, as now, the Arabs maintained that the Jews had no right to any portion of the holy city.

In the 1948 War of Independence the Arabs were unsuccessful in taking the whole of Jerusalem. They were able to retain only the Old City and portions of East Jerusalem. Thus, from 1948 to 1967, the city was divided, separating Arabs and Jews, families and friends by walls and barbed wire.

Crossing from one section of the city to the other was not an easy task prior to 1967. Jews were strictly forbidden entrance to East Jerusalem and to the Old City. Others who crossed the city's Arab/Jewish border, mostly tourists, were required to pass through the Mandelbaum Gate, not far from the Damascus Gate. While Jordan permitted tourists to enter West Jerusalem from their side, they would not permit entrance from Jewish Jerusalem. Tourists who desired to visit the Old City between 1948 and 1967 were required to enter Old Jerusalem from Jordanian territory. Tourists traveling to Jordan with an Israeli stamp in their passports were denied entrance. This practice was the same in most other Arab countries as well.

Everything changed in Jerusalem in 1967 when Israel seized control of the Old City and East Jerusalem. The barbed wire and barriers separating the city's two sections were removed. Arabs, Jews and tourists were permitted to travel freely within the city. Holy places in all sections of Jerusalem were opened to everyone. Israel has gone to great lengths to protect the holy places of all faiths and to promote free access by all pilgrims.

While there have been many incidents of protest and terrorism in Jerusalem since 1967, the city's Arabs and Jews have lived quite peaceably, each in their own designated neighborhoods. The Arabs living in Israel today, contrary to certain propaganda, have a significantly higher standard of living than Arabs living in neighboring countries. Teddy Kollek, mayor of Jerusalem, has been instrumental for over twenty years in cultivating better relations between Jews and Arabs. There are extremists on both sides who would like to see the other completely exiled from the country. Fortunately, these extremist views are a minority.

The history of West Jerusalem dates to 1860 when Sir Moses Montefiore built the first Jewish community outside the walls of Old Jerusalem and called it Mishkenot Sha'Ananim (meaning "Dwelling of Tranquil Ones). An old windmill, now a landmark of Jerusalem and dedicated to the memory of Montefiore, founder of modern Jerusalem, is located near the King David Hotel.

West Jerusalem is a beautiful and vibrant city with a population of nearly 500,000. Its new buildings constructed with native stone blend with the older structures. The majority of Jerusalem's residents live in apartment buildings, though there are numerous single family homes as well. Tall and impressive buildings silhouette Jerusalem's skyline, giving it the appearance of a growing and progressive city. In recent years, many modern hotels have been constructed in Jerusalem to accommodate the more than one million tourists who visit each year. Most of Israel's government buildings are plain and unpretentious; however, the stately Knesset building is the centerpiece of new Jerusalem. Office buildings, banks, and other business concerns are housed in structures not unlike those of other modern cities. Noise, pollution, traffic, and other urban problems are fast becoming common in this ancient capital as well.

At 2500 feet above sea level, Jerusalem's cool climate offers guests

The Shrine of the Book and the Knesset viewed from the grounds of the Israel Museum.

and residents a very pleasant environment. While the summer days may be hot and dry, the evenings are usually cool and comfortable. Rain is plentiful in the winter months (November - March), and occasionally a blanket of snow covers the city, gracing its beauty in white and causing it unaccustomed traffic problems. While flowers bloom throughout the year in Jerusalem, springtime is a feast for the eyes. Then the flowers and trees are at their peak of perfection, the hills are arrayed in various shades of green, and Jerusalem's beauty is unsurpassed.

THE KNESSET

Israel's parliament building, the Knesset (meaning "assembly" in Hebrew), is beautifully situated on a lofty hillside overlooking the Hebrew University and the Israel Museum. Other government buildings nearby include: the Ministry of Finance, the Ministry of Interior, the Ministry of Labor and Welfare, and the office of the Prime Minister. Because of the heavy burden of taxation borne by Israeli citizens, many locals refer to the treasury building as the "second wailing wall."

Israel's national assembly is composed of 120 members, men and women who are elected to four year terms by popular vote. The majority party in the Knesset forms the administrative government which is led by a prime minister. While Israel has a president, his functions are primarily ceremonial. Since no political party has ever gained a clear majority in Israeli elections, all governments have been formed through coalitions of political parties. Most times these coalitions are compositions of differing political viewpoints and ideologies, making Israel's politics interesting as well as noisy. Debates in the Knesset are conducted in Hebrew and open to the public; many are televised. Arabs living in Israel have been granted full citizenship and are represented in the Knesset, too.

Inside the Knesset building itself are some outstanding works of modern art, including mosaics and tapestries by Marc Chagall. Visitors who enter the building are required to pass through very strict security. Opposite the main entrance of the Knesset is a large menorah, a gift to the people of Israel from Great Britain.

The Isaiah Scroll beneath the Shrine of the Book's lid-shaped roof.

THE SHRINE OF THE BOOK

A short distance from the Knesset on the grounds of the Israel Museum is an oddly-shaped building called the Shrine of the Book. In it are housed a portion of the Dead Sea Scrolls, along with many artifacts which were found in the area of the Dead Sea. Since the Dead Sea Scrolls were discovered in clay jars hidden away in caves, the main building is modeled after a cave, while its roof has been made to resemble the lid of a clay jar. The entire building is climatized to protect the valuable artifacts and scrolls. The thickness of the structure itself offers protection in case of war or earthquake.

In the center of the museum, directly under the lid-shaped ceiling, is a copy of the scroll of Isaiah found in the caves of Qumran in 1947. The scroll which measures thirty-four feet in length is hundreds of years older than any other existing copy of Isaiah. With only a few insignificant exceptions, the text is identical to later existing copies of Isaiah. The ancient Dead Sea manuscripts give clear evidence to the authenticity and integrity of our present Scriptures.

THE HEBREW UNIVERSITY

Because the original campus of the Hebrew University on Mount Scopus became inaccessible after Israel's War of Independence, a new campus was constructed in West Jerusalem. This large and attractive campus served well for a number of years, but more space was required as the University grew. After Israel captured East Jerusalem in 1967, work was begun on the restoration of the Mount Scopus campus where currently over 10,000 students are housed. The Hebrew University with its more than 20,000 students is known throughout the world for academic excellence.

THE HADASSAH MEDICAL CENTER

The most outstanding medical facility in the Middle East is the Hadassah Medical Center, built on the outskirts of West Jerusalem just beyond the little village of Ein Karem. In addition to a world-renowned center of research, it also includes a training center for

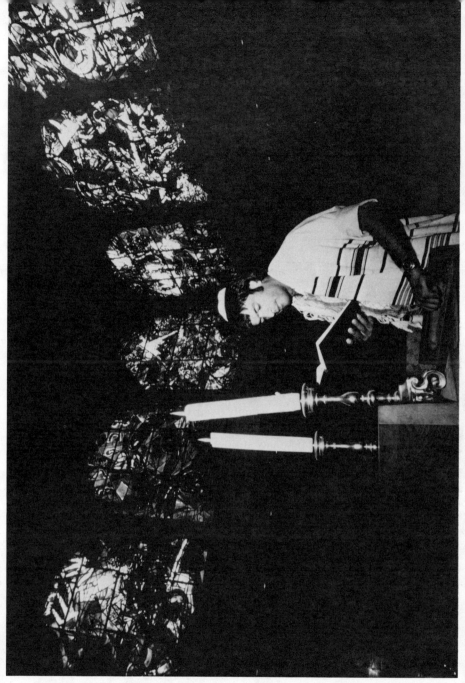

Jewish man at prayer beneath Marc Chagall's windows in the synagogue of the Hadassah Hospital near Ein Karem.

doctors, nurses and various medical technicians. The hospital which treats both Arab and Jew has 800 beds and a staff of 2300.

A modern synagogue in the hospital complex has twelve windows created by Marc Chagall. Thousands of visitors tour the hospital and see these famous, brightly colored stained glass windows which are rich in biblical symbolism centering around the twelve tribes of Jacob.

Israel lost access to the old Hadassah Hospital complex on Mount Scopus together with the Hebrew University from 1948 to 1967. The new hospital in West Jerusalem has been augmented through the reconstruction of the old facilities on Mount Scopus following the Six Day War.

THE KENNEDY MEMORIAL

John F. Kennedy, thirty-fifth President of the United States and a good friend to Israel, is honored by an impressive memorial erected a short distance west of Jerusalem on Mount Orah. The Kennedy Memorial was financed through contributions from citizens of every state in the Union.

The lines of the building actually begin on the pavement surrounding the memorial. They flow to the base of fifty-one columns which sweep upward until they are abruptly cut off, symbolizing the untimely death of the young President. Inside, glass panels between the columns complete the circular wall which offers a panoramic view of the Judean hills and the John F. Kennedy Peace Forest adjacent to the memorial. Mounted separately on the interior of the fifty-one columns are the seals of each of the fifty states and the District of Columbia. An eternal flame burns beneath a relief-portrait of Kennedy.

YAD VASHEM

No visit to Israel would be complete without experiencing the memorial to the six million Jews who perished in the Holocaust. Yad Vashem is more than a memorial. It is also a museum of the Holocaust and a depository of names and information about millions of Jews who died at the hands of the Nazis. Established in 1957, the memorial stands atop the Mount of Remembrance, a short distance from Mount Herzl. Most of the victims of the Holocaust were burned to ashes or buried in unmarked graves. Yad Vashem now offers them a dignity in death which they were denied in life. The Hebrew words *Yad Vashem* (meaning "a memorial and a name") come from the book of Isaiah:

> . . . to them I will give within my temple
> and its walls a memorial and a name,
> better than sons and daughters; I will
> give them an everlasting name that will
> not be cut off (56:5).

In the archives of the Martyrs and Heroes Remembrance Authority are photos, films, letters, documents, books, and various artifacts of the Holocaust. The Institute has undertaken to gather all the names of the six million slain. Since entire Jewish communities and families were completely exterminated, the task of locating names is most difficult. Currently less than half of the six million Jews have been identified. Those names have been preserved in the Hall of Names, dedicated in November 1977.

The museum at Yad Vashem displays pictures, documents, and artifacts of the Holocaust in a most understated fashion. Few words are spoken by visitors as images of the Holocaust are indelibly seared on their minds and consciences. Markers on the floor in the Hall of Remembrance list the various Nazi death camps, while an eternal flame pays silent tribute to the memory of the six million people who posthumously have been made honorary citizens of Israel. Only the dead in heart could fail to be moved at Yad Vashem.

A tall column outside the Hall of Remembrance symbolizes a smokestack from the crematoriums. Other sculptures and works of art on the grounds of Yad Vashem offer symbolic tribute to individual acts of bravery during the Holocaust. A grove of trees is dedicated to Gentiles who aided and protected Jews from the Nazi atrocities.

The newest addition to Yad Vashem is The Children's Memorial, dedicated to the 1,500,000 children who perished in the Holocaust. Five continuously burning candles are reflected thousands of times through a network of 500 mirrors placed on the floor, walls and ceiling. The names of individual children who perished in the Holocaust are read simultaneously as their pictures are illuminated from the darkness.

Near an exit of the museum is a plaque which reads:

FORGETFULNESS LEADS TO EXILE,
WHILE REMEMBRANCE IS THE SECRET OF
REDEMPTION.

Indeed, it is extremely painful to reflect upon all the images of death and suffering which so ignominiously assaulted the entire Jewish community in Europe, but God forbid that the world ever forgets such gross inhumanity. Perhaps the greatest tribute of all to the six million slain is not found in the buildings, halls or monuments of Yad Vashem, but rather in the tears of those who go there and *remember*.

EIN KAREM

Nestled in a deep valley not far from Yad Vashem is the village of Ein Karem where tradition alleges that John the Baptist was born. Two Franciscan churches recall important biblical events from his life. The Church of Saint John is built over a grotto where Catholics believe that Elizabeth gave birth to John. On a nearby hillside, built over the traditional summer residence of Zachariah and Elizabeth, is the Church of the Visitation. The Franciscans believe that here the Virgin Mary visited Zachariah and Elizabeth prior to the birth of Jesus.

THE MODEL CITY OF JERUSALEM

On the grounds of the Holy Land Hotel in West Jerusalem is a scale model of Jerusalem as it appeared in 66 A.D. Built of white limestone, the superbly detailed model affords visitors a better understanding of the city in the time of Christ. The model also serves as an excellent resource to comprehend the topography, location and relationship of the various biblical sites. Completed in 1969, the Model City was planned by Professor Michael Avi-Yonah.

Memorial sculpture at Yad Vashem.

Recorded English commentary is available to the visitors along the walkway surrounding the model.

ISRAEL'S NATIONAL CEMETERY

The Mount Herzl Cemetery is situated in West Jerusalem, not far from Yad Vashem. Many prominent Israelis have been laid to rest in this lovely and tranquil setting. Located at the highest point of the cemetery is the grave of Theodor Herzl, father of modern Israel. A large black-marble stone marks his resting place. Golda Meir, former prime minister of Israel, is buried here also.

One area of the cemetery incorporates a shallow pool of water, a memorial to 140 soldiers of the 402nd Jewish Transport Unit who perished in 1943 when their ship was sunk in the Mediterranean Sea. There are also special areas for the fallen of various wars in Israel's history. It is a deeply moving experience to walk the tree-lined paths which entwine this historic cemetery.

ישראל

ISRAEL

From Bethlehem to Eilat

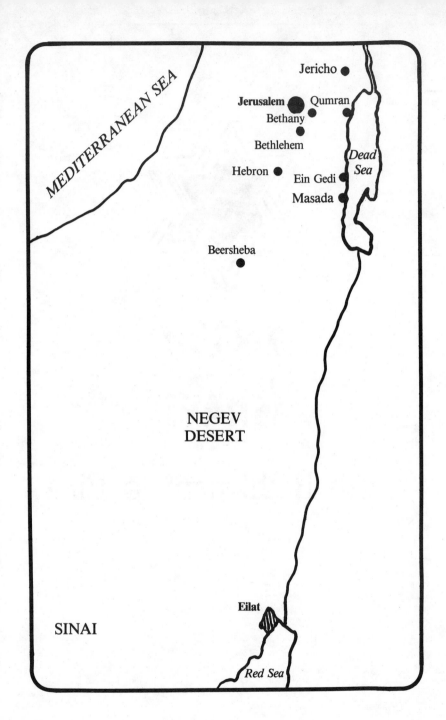

From Bethlehem To Eilat

BETHLEHEM

The little town of David where Christ was born is only six miles south of Jerusalem on the occupied West Bank. Bethlehem (meaning "house of bread" in Hebrew) is an Arab community of some 15,000 residents.

Bethlehem was home to Ruth and Boaz, great-grandparents of King David. After her husband and father-in-law died, Ruth left her own land of Moab with her mother-in-law, Naomi, who was returning to Bethlehem following a lengthy sojourn. Later Ruth married Boaz. Interestingly, the mountains of Moab are visible from Bethlehem on the eastern horizon.

David was born in Bethlehem, and on its many hilly slopes he tended his father's sheep. In Bethlehem, Samuel annointed David to succeed Saul as king of Israel (1 Samuel 16:1-13). But, of course, Bethlehem's chief claim to fame is as the birthplace of Jesus. Hundreds of years before the birth of Christ, Micah wrote:

> But you, Bethlehem Ephrathah, though you are small among the clans of Judah, out of you will come for me one who will be ruler over Israel, whose origins are from of old, from ancient times (5:2).

The Church of the Nativity, the oldest church structure in the world, stands over the grotto where it is believed that Jesus was born. Adjacent to the church is a large parking lot known as Manger Square. Nearby is Shepherds' Field, the traditional site of the angelic announcement regarding Jesus' birth to the humble Bethlehem shepherds.

If one ventures into the side streets of Bethlehem, a more primitive array of stores and shops may be experienced. Arab women in native dress, some carrying large burdens on their heads, walk about the streets tending to family shopping. Some of the townsmen may be observed sitting in the storefronts and smoking their water pipes as they watch the passers-by. Bethlehem's shops are filled with olive-wood carvings and mother-of-pearl jewelry fashioned by local industry. Tourism is Bethlehem's chief commerce. In many ways, the shops and bazaars of Bethlehem are as interesting as those in Jerusalem's Old City.

THE CHURCH OF THE NATIVITY

The traditional birthplace of Jesus is found in a cave beneath the main altar of the Church of the Nativity. The original structure, dedicated by Queen Helena in 339, was enlarged in the sixth century. The Crusaders fortified the building, giving it the appearance of a castle. To keep Moslems from riding into the church on horseback, the Crusaders sealed a large portion of the main archway, leaving only a tiny door for entry. Later the Turks made the opening even smaller in an effort to prevent looting. To enter the Church today one must bend his knees, which seems more than a little appropriate.

Through centuries of use, two deep grooves have been worn into the stone threshold of the church's main entrance. The greatest and least of saints and sinners have entered the church on bended-knee. It is a humbling experience to join their ranks as pilgrims to this most holy and authentic site.

A double row of pink-limestone Corinthian pillars adorn the rather plain nave. The wooden roof with its exposed beams was constructed in the fifteenth century. Through trap doors in the present floor one may observe a beautiful mosaic floor from the original fourth-century church. Large chandeliers hang from the ceiling, and a magnificent screen secludes the main altar. An active Greek Orthodox congregation regularly worships here.

To the right and left of the main altar are steps leading down to the Grotto of the Nativity. (Grotto is Latin for "cave.") An Orthodox priest is usually stationed near the steps to seek an offering. In re-

The Church of the Nativity in Bethlehem, the world's oldest church.

turn, he offers the pilgrims a devotional candle to place at the site of the nativity.

The grotto is ten feet high, forty feet long, and ten feet wide. Tapestries hang from the walls in the dark and gloomy cave. A silver star on the floor marks the traditional place where Mary gave birth to Jesus. Around the star are the Latin words *Hic de Virgine Maria Jesus Christus Natus Est* (meaning "Here of the Virgin Mary, Jesus Christ was born"). Nearby, beneath an altar regularly used for mass, is the manger. (The Roman Catholics claim that the original manger is in the Church of Saint Mary Major in Rome.)

The grotto is often crowded as priests celebrate mass and hundreds of pilgrims seek a brief look at this holy site. Protestants are not accorded much consideration at this and many other places in the Holy Land. They may have their devotionals in the grotto only when it is not being occupied by the priests. Yet one's heart is moved to be near the place where the Word "became flesh and dwelt among us."

Near the top of the stairs leading from the grotto is a small portion of the church controlled by the Armenians who share this ancient basilica with the Roman Catholics and the Greek Orthodox. Beyond the Armenian section is the Roman Catholic Church of Saint Catherine. It is from this beautiful sanctuary that the traditional Christmas Eve mass is celebrated and broadcast around the world via modern communication networks.

THE HOME OF SAINT JEROME

Stairs descend from Saint Catherine's nave to the subterranean home of Saint Jerome. Jerome, one of the early church fathers, sought to live and work as close as possible to the site of the nativity. An advocate of the monastic life, he lived there for thirty-four years. Jerome is best known for his translation of the Scriptures into Latin (Vulgate). He died in his Bethlehem home on September 30, 420.

Catherine, whose name the Roman Catholic portion of the Church bears, suffered martyrdom on a spiked wheel. The symbol of the spiked wheel is used repeatedly inside the sanctuary. Her remains are in Saint Catherine's Church on Mount Sinai.

SHEPHERDS' FIELD

The locations for almost every major event in the Bible, as well as many minor ones, have been identified at some point in time in the Holy Land, with or without substantiation. The Greek Orthodox site at the outskirts of Bethlehem called "Shepherds' Field" is one which fits the latter category. It is impossible to know the precise location where the angels announced their glad tidings to the shepherds. Yet it is certain that it was at such a place as this and very close at hand. Today shepherds still tend their flocks around Shepherds' Field. Somewhere in the same area David tended his father's sheep, and Ruth gleaned behind the reapers in the fields of Boaz.

Unlike the crowded and busy Church of the Nativity, pilgrims are seldom hurried or bothered at Shepherds' Field, making it an appropriate place for worship and praise. Truly this pastoral setting has changed little from the time of Christ. The Roman Catholics also have a site which they regard as Shepherds' Field.

RACHEL'S TOMB

Rachel's Tomb, an ancient shrine located at the outskirts of Bethlehem, is extremely holy to the Jews. While traveling to Hebron with her husband, Jacob, and his eleven sons, Rachel died near Bethlehem after giving birth to Benjamin. Jacob buried his beloved Rachel near the place of her death. The beautiful love story of Jacob and Rachel, recorded in Genesis 29, may be summed up in one brief sentence: "So Jacob served seven years to get Rachel, but they seemed like only a few days to him because of his love for her" (verse 20).

HERODIUM

Three and a half miles southeast of Bethlehem are the ruins of Herodium, another of Herod the Great's unique building projects. This fortress-palace was erected in 23 B.C. upon an artificial hill which the historian Josephus said "resembled a woman's breast." Two hundred white-marble steps were built to give access to the summit where Herod constructed a double wall, incorporating three

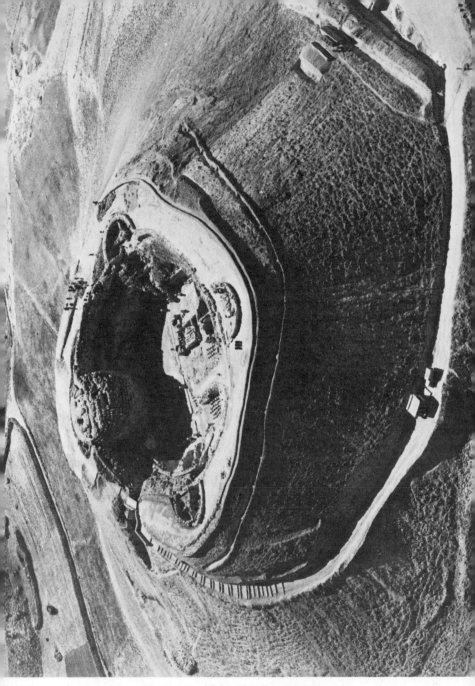

Herodium, King Herod's fortress-palace built in 23 B.C.

semi-circular towers and one round tower. Within the walls were palaces and many other elaborate buildings. According to historical accounts, Herod was buried at Herodium on a solid gold bier studded with precious stones. However, his tomb has never been found.

Jewish rebels from the First Revolt occupied Herodium for a considerable period of time, but finally were overrun by the advancing Roman army. Recent excavations have revealed that Herodium was used also in the Second Jewish Revolt (132–135) by Bar-Kokhba and his followers. Many coins and documents from the Second Revolt were discovered here, as well as an elaborate underground tunnel system.

HEBRON

One of the oldest continuously inhabited cities of Palestine is Hebron, located twenty miles southeast of Jerusalem. Approximately 3,000 feet above sea level, Hebron is an Arab community, though in recent years numerous Jewish settlements have been established here. The Scriptures reveal that Hebron was built seven years before Zoan of Egypt (1720 B.C.). Excavations in the area offer evidence that an earlier town dating to 3300 B.C. might have existed here as well.

Hebron is mentioned fifty times in the Old Testament. Abraham resided in Hebron after he and Lot separated (Genesis 13:18). Abraham's wife, Sarah, was buried here (Genesis 23:1). Jacob sent his son, Joseph, to Shechem from Hebron to find his brothers and check on their welfare. Later his brothers returned home to Hebron after they had dipped Joseph's colorful coat in blood to convince Jacob that Joseph was dead when, in fact, they had sold him into slavery (Genesis 37).

The spies sent into Canaan by Moses returned from the Hebron area with a single cluster of grapes so large that they carried it on a pole between two men (Numbers 13:22–24). Only two of the spies, Joshua and Caleb, believed that the land could be taken by the Israelites. Because of his great faith that the children of Israel could go up immediately and possess the Promised Land, Caleb was given the city as his possession (Judges 1:20). Joshua destroyed Hebron in his conquest of the Promised Land (Joshua 10:36–37).

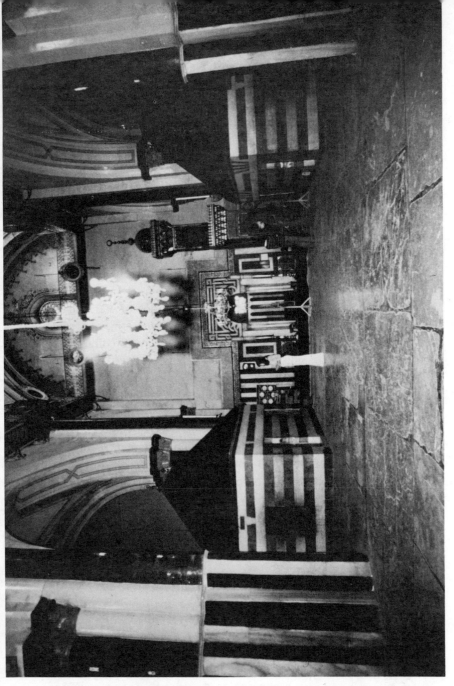

The Mosque of Abraham, built over the ancient Cave of Machpelah where the Patriarchs and their wives are buried.

King David reigned in Hebron for seven and a half years before moving his capital to Jerusalem (2 Samuel 5:1-5). Absalom, David's son, conspired from his Hebron birthplace to take the throne from his father (2 Samuel 15). King Rehoboam fortified the city of Hebron (2 Chronicles 11:10).

The city was captured by Judas Maccabeus. During the First Jewish Revolt, it was destroyed by the Romans. When Saladin took Hebron from the Crusaders in 1187, it became an important Arab stronghold. However, until the riots of 1929, there had always been a Jewish community living there. Today Hebron is part of the occupied West Bank, under the control of Israel since 1967.

The most outstanding place of interest in Hebron is the Mosque of Abraham (Harem el-Khalil), built over the ancient Cave of Machpelah. Abraham purchased the cave from Ephron the Hittite for 400 shekels of silver as a burial place for his wife, Sarah (Genesis 23). Abraham and Sarah, Isaac and Rebecca, Jacob and Leah were buried here. The present Mosque of Abraham was originally a Crusader church built over the ruins of a sixth-century basilica. Around the mosque is a large enclosure, 213 feet by 115 feet, the lower portion built by Herod the Great. In the mosque is a pulpit brought from Egypt by Saladin. The Cave of Machpelah is located below the mosque and has not been entered since Crusader times.

BEERSHEBA

More than any other city in Israel, Beersheba exemplifies the Israelis' technical development of a progressive and productive homeland. Known as the capital of the Negev, Beersheba is a Jewish city with a population of over 110,000. Prior to 1948 it was only a small desert town. The city takes great pride in its impressive industrial complex, a new university, a beautiful cultural center, and a modern hospital. A research center established at Beersheba in 1957 contributes practical scientific data to the development of desert resources such as solar energy, desalination of water, soil development, geology, biology, and artificial rainmaking. Uniquely designed housing and commercial buildings take into consideration the desert conditions.

At the turn of the twentieth century, the Turks established an administrative headquarters at Beersheba to govern the Negev Bedouin tribes. The first town taken from the Turks by the British in 1917 was Beersheba. The Egyptians controlled the city briefly following the War of Independence, but they were driven out by Israel in a special action on October 21, 1948. Reacting to various truce violations on the part of Egypt, Israel launched "Operation Ten Plagues" which sent Egyptian forces in the area retreating, except for twenty-five thousand troops surrounded by Israeli forces. Among those trapped soldiers was Gamal Abdel Nasser.

Excavations conducted by the University of Tel Aviv in the Beersheba area from 1954 to 1971 revealed that an ancient civilization dwelt here between 4,000 and 3,000 B.C. The city was known in Scriptures as the dwelling place of the Patriarchs. At Beersheba Abraham made an oath with Abimelech regarding water rights, and afterwards planted a tamarisk tree to mark the place (Genesis 21:25–33). Likewise, Isaac made a covenant with Abimelech at Beersheba (Genesis 26:23–33). After his famous deception and quarrel with his brother, Esau, young Jacob left Beersheba and journeyed to the home of his Uncle Laban in Haran (Genesis 28:10).

Beersheba was assigned to the tribe of Simeon (Joshua 19:2). It was the southernmost city at the time of the Judges as shown in the expression, "from Dan to Beersheba" (Judges 20:1). It was here that Samuel made his sons, Joel and Abijah, judges over Israel (1 Samuel 8:1-3). The prophet Elijah fled to Beersheba from the wicked Queen Jezebel (1 Kings 19:1-3).

The Negev's Bedouins still use this modern Jewish city as a center for trade and marketing. The Bedouin market in Beersheba is a most interesting attraction for residents and tourists alike. A considerable number of the Bedouins have given up the nomadic life and built homes in this area.

EILAT

Eilat is a small port in comparison to Haifa, but its location on the Red Sea is most strategic. In addition to being the southernmost city in modern Israel, Eilat offers access from the Gulf of Aqaba to the Indian Ocean and the Orient. The land on which the city stands was

Unique formations along the shore of the Dead Sea.

captured on March 10, 1949 in one of the last actions of the War of Independence. The city itself was not established until 1950.

Eilat was known in the Scriptures as Elath (from Elah, meaning terebinth tree). The people of Israel passed here as they journeyed from Egypt to the Promised Land (Deuteronomy 2:8). Elath and nearby Ezion-Geber are mentioned as important ports during the days of Solomon (1 Kings 9:26). Archaeological excavations in the area have unearthed ruins of an ancient civilization.

Approximately fifteen miles north of Eilat are Solomon's Mines which produced significant quantities of copper until recent years. Also, in and around the city are several small industries. However, the most significant industry of this constantly growing city is tourism.

Without the tourists, Eilat's population numbers about 17,500. But, twelve months out of the year, thousands more crowd the city's many hotels to enjoy the area's outstanding attractions. In the winter months the warm sun and the sandy beaches are very appealing, but even in the hot summer months the hotels report an eighty percent capacity. Glass-bottom boats open an enchanting vista to the wonders of the Red Sea, while a newly built aquarium (Coral World) delights young and old with a marvelous display of exotic fish.

The cost of living is high in Eilat, because everything has to be shipped, hauled or flown into the city since it is so far from the center of the country where goods and services are readily available. In order to convince people to settle there, the government of Israel once offered tax incentives to new settlers. A few years ago one of Eilat's leading financiers built an extensive housing project containing 200 expensive villas and 150 vacation apartments.

Eilat's security was frequently threatened in the past. Egypt closed the Straits of Teran in 1956 and 1967, blocking any access to the Red Sea. Israel captured the area in the Sinai War of 1956, but returned it when navigation rights were assured by the international community. After a subsequent blockade by Egypt in 1967, Israel captured the entire Sinai again and firmly established herself in the Straits of Teran at the city of Sharm el-Sheikh. The Sinai was returned to Egypt again following the signing of the peace treaty in 1979.

ישראל

ISRAEL

On The Jericho Road

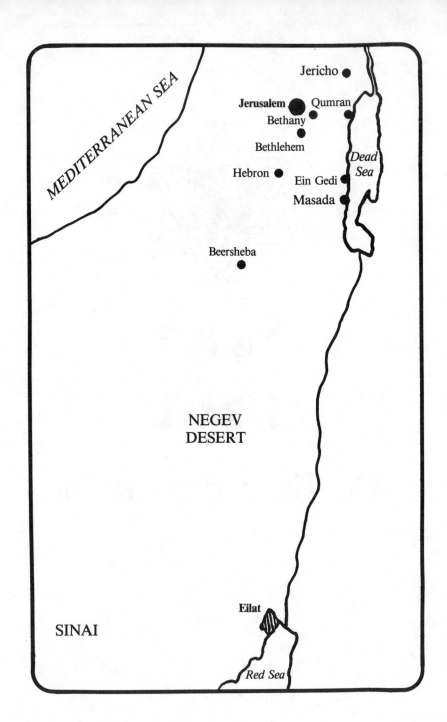

On The Jericho Road

Only a few ruins remain of the ancient road leading from Jerusalem to Jericho. In the days of Jesus the road was little more than a footpath winding up the Mount of Olives to Bethany before meandering through the barren hills of the Judean desert. On that lonely and dangerous stretch of road many travelers were robbed, beaten and victimized by hordes of bandits. This fact was the setting for Christ's parable of the Good Samaritan (Luke 10). Jesus' words, "A man was going down from Jerusalem to Jericho, and he fell among robbers . . . ", take on added significance as the treacherous terrain is viewed. Even Jesus' use of the word *down* is better understood when traveling from Jerusalem which is 2700 feet above sea level to Jericho which is 820 feet below sea level.

A day's journey in Bible times takes only thirty minutes today by auto on a modern highway. The desert hills have a rugged beauty which is little changed from the time of Christ. Dry wadi beds cut through the hills reveal the intensity of the water run-off during the winter rains. From the road one often sees shepherds leading their flocks over the hills in search of the few grassy areas available. Likely the traveler also will see Bedouin families camped in their black goatskin tents among the hills. The nomadic Bedouins lead a most primitive lifestyle, seemingly oblivious to the modern world around them, except for an occasional television aerial jutting from a tent or shack.

Donkeys grazing along the road or up in the hills are sometimes seen by the observant traveler, as well as camels closer to the Dead Sea. The Israeli military camps and gun emplacements dug into the hillsides of this West Bank territory tell a modern story of this ancient desert region.

BETHANY

According to the New Testament, the Jericho Road was traversed several times by Jesus and His disciples. There are several reports of occasions when Jesus stopped in Bethany to visit the home of His friends, Lazarus, Mary and Martha. Bethany (meaning "house of poverty" in Aramaic) is an Arab village situated two miles from Jerusalem on the eastern slopes of the Mount of Olives.

There are two primary places of interest in Bethany, a Franciscan church and a first-century tomb. The Church of Lazarus is built over the traditional site of his home; the tomb is supposedly the one from which Lazarus was raised from the dead by Jesus (John 11).

It was at the home of Simon the leper in Bethany that Mary, sister of Martha and Lazarus, poured a jar of costly perfume on the feet of Jesus just prior to His crucifixion. Judas Iscariot voiced his strong disapproval of Mary's seemingly wasteful act (John 12:1-8).

Surely our greatest legacy from Jesus' visits to Bethany is found not at the tomb or even in the lovely Franciscan church with its beautiful mosaics, but rather in the words which Jesus spoke at Bethany just prior to Lazarus being raised from the dead. These words unquestionably constitute one of the greatest messages ever spoken by God to man:

> I AM THE RESURRECTION AND THE LIFE.
> HE WHO BELIEVES IN ME WILL LIVE,
> EVEN THOUGH HE DIES;
> AND WHOEVER LIVES AND BELIEVES IN ME
> WILL NEVER DIE
>
> *(John 11:25–26)*.

On the Mount of Olives and near the tomb of Lazarus were many other graves and tombs. Because Jesus is the Lord of Life, it is possible that He spoke Lazarus' name specifically for good reason; otherwise, every dead person buried on the Mount of Olives might have obeyed His summons to "come forth." Believing Jesus' words of John 11: 25-26, we Christians also live in the hope that one day we shall hear the Master's voice call us from the grave to resurrection and life eternal.

THE INN OF THE GOOD SAMARITAN

Not far from Bethany on a section of the old Jericho Road stands a building known as the Inn of the Good Samaritan. The building is from the Turkish period, and was used as a police station. Though definitely not authentic, the building and its location give insight into Christ's parable as recorded in Luke 10:29–37.

INTO THE JORDAN VALLEY

The road approaching the Jordan Valley from Jerusalem forks northward to Jericho and southward to Qumran and Masada. The Mountains of Moab rise majestically beyond the Jordan River in the Hashemite Kingdom of Jordan. Easily seen among the peaks of the Moab mountain range is Mount Nebo where Moses was permitted to view the Promised Land, though God would not allow him to enter.

JERICHO

The modern town of Jericho is an Arab community on the West Bank, controlled by Israel since 1967. The town is quite busy and prosperous with its tropical and sub-tropical fruit and vegetable farms. Riding through the tree-shaded streets of Jericho with its citrus groves, one is reminded of a town in Florida. The weather in Jericho is pleasant in the winter months, but during the summer it becomes extremely hot. A visit to Jericho would not be complete without stopping for refreshment at one of the many fruit stands.

At the edge of modern Jericho are excavations of Old Testament and Caananite Jericho. Begun in 1907, these excavations revealed a city which existed centuries before Joshua. In fact, Jericho may be the world's oldest continuing city. A massive trench exposes an ancient stone tower which some archaeologists date beyond 7,000 B.C. The excavations further reveal that the city was destroyed and rebuilt many times.

From the top of the excavations of ancient Jericho, one has a magnificent view of the lush and green Jordan Valley. The Mount of Temptation, seen in the opposite direction, towers above the Jordan Valley. This marks the traditional location of Jesus' temptation in the wilderness as recorded in the Gospel (Luke 4:1-13). A monastery on the cliff-like side of the Mount of Temptation is barely visible from below.

Approximately two miles from the modern city of Jericho is the Jericho of New Testament times. It was common in the days of Jesus for Jews in the Galilee to travel to Jerusalem via Jericho in order to avoid passing through Samaria. On one occasion when Jesus traveled through Jericho on His way to Jerusalem, the tax collector, Zacchaeus, much hated by his fellow townsmen, received Jesus into his home and into his heart. After his encounter with Jesus, Zacchaeus was a new man (Luke 19:1-10). Another desperate soul who met Jesus in Jericho was blind Bartimaeus. After meeting Jesus he was blind no longer (Mark 10:46–52).

A site of interest near Jericho is Hisham's Palace, located one mile north of Old Testament Jericho. The ruins are recognized as a winter home of Caliph Hisham and date to 724 A.D. In the same general area are the ruins of a fifth-century A.D. synagogue with one of the most outstanding mosaic floors yet discovered in Israel.

THE DEAD SEA

The Dead Sea, nine miles south of Jericho, has an apt name for a large body of water with little or no organic life. On a clear day it is visible from certain areas of Jerusalem. Its deep blue water contrasted against the nearby hills and rugged mountains presents a scene of incomparable beauty.

The principal source of water for the Dead Sea is the Jordan River, though also fed by waters running off the Judean hills and the Moab Mountains in winter months. The Dead Sea, forty-eight miles long and ten miles wide (average), has no outlet. Much of its water is lost through evaporation. On the shores of the Dead Sea one stands at the lowest point of the earth's surface, about 1292 feet below sea level. The western half of this mineral sea belongs to Israel; the eastern half belongs to Jordan.

The value of the minerals contained in the Dead Sea is nearly beyond calculation. These minerals include: sodium, calcium, potassium, magnesium, bromine, chlorine and sulphate. Industries producing many of these minerals are increasingly important to Israel's economy. Presently these represent about 10 percent of the nation's industrial exports.

The tourist industry has also begun to flourish on the shores of the Dead Sea. Resort hotels, health spas, restaurants and beaches cater to Israeli and foreign tourists. People seeking relief from skin conditions, rheumatism, arthritis and old age enjoy bathing in the warm mineral-rich waters. On a cool winter day residents of Jerusalem may travel the forty-minute distance to bask in the balmy breezes of the Dead Sea.

Along the shores of this arid region are numerous Israeli settlements and kibbutzim where winter vegetables and sub-tropical fruits are successfully grown.

QUMRAN

The most important archaeological discovery of modern times occurred in 1947 at Qumran near the shore of the Dead Sea. A Bedouin shepherd boy accidently discovered a cave containing several clay jars filled with old scrolls. The initial find led to an extensive archaeological search which produced the now world-famous Dead Sea Scrolls. In addition, other documents and artifacts from the first century A.D. were garnered from the innumerable caves of Qumran. The scrolls, wrapped in cloth and placed in large clay jars, were protected by the dry climate of the Dead Sea area. Ironically, these valuable documents were preserved in an environment which has been known to kill a man in less than a day.

The scrolls and artifacts were hidden by a religious society known as the Essenes. They settled at Qumran about 100 B.C. to retreat from the world and to devote themselves to study and prayer. Excavations conducted between 1951 and 1956 revealed an organized and self-sufficient community. The Essene complex included a watch tower, a large room for study and writing (scriptorium), a kitchen, dining room, ritual baths, and water reservoirs.

In 68 A.D. the Roman army destroyed Qumran. But, in advance of their destruction, the Essenes gathered their scrolls and other valuables and carefully hid them away in nearby caves. Those documents and artifacts remained hidden for nearly two thousand years. It seems more than a coincidence that they would be hidden at the very time the Jews were being scattered to the ends of the earth and discovered two millennia later in the very year that the nation of Israel was officially restored. Surely these historical documents were preserved by God Himself as He continues to shape the history and destiny of His people.

One complete copy and one incomplete copy of Isaiah were found. These manuscripts have been dated from l00 B.C. to l00 A.D. Also discovered was the "Manual of Discipline" used to govern the Essene community. These, as well as many other fragments, were collected and placed in Israel's museums. The most outstanding discovery was in Cave #4 which contained over four hundred manuscripts and some scraps of papyrus. This great archaeological find has added much insight to biblical studies and has helped scholars to better comprehend the various religious and political influences of first-century Palestine.

EIN GEDI

The scenery along the shores of the Dead Sea is magnificent, especially when the sun and sky are reflected on the shimmering waters beneath the rugged desert hills. While tranquil in appearance, the area is filled with dangers, as many unsuspecting travelers have discovered. Temperatures which often reach l25 degrees and higher in the summer months can cause an unprotected person to die in only a few hours. Though the region receives little rainfall, swift torrents of water often sweep down from the Judean Desert during the heavy winter rains. Flash floods have often washed out the roads, sending cars, people and huge boulders into the Dead Sea without warning. It staggers one's imagination to comprehend such flooding in the desert.

But all is not barren wilderness along the Dead Sea. An oasis dating to Biblical times rises defiantly amidst the desolation. The oasis is Ein Gedi (Hebrew for "Spring of the Kid"). David fled to Ein Gedi when King Saul was trying to kill him (1 Samuel 24:1-3). Ein Gedi is also mentioned in Song of Solomon 1:14 and in Ezekiel 47:10.

A large and prosperous kibbutz has been established at Ein Gedi. In addition to agricultural projects, the kibbutz members operate a modern inn and restaurant. A stop at the restaurant gives visitors an opportunity to relax and enjoy a swim in the salty waters of the Dead Sea.

It was near Ein Gedi that important archaeological finds from the Bar-Kokhba Revolt were made. Bar-Kokhba led a revolt against Emperor Hadrian between 132 and 135 A.D. Hadrian had attempted to establish a pronounced Roman influence in Jerusalem, changing its name to Aelia Capitolina. His actions so outraged the Jews still living there that, under the leadership of Simon Bar-Kokhba, they successfully forced the Romans from the city. For a time, the Jews established their own government, but in less than three years the revolt was crushed by twelve Roman legions. Many of Bar-Kokhba's followers retreated to the hills and caves at Ein Gedi where they were finally captured or killed. An important archaeological expedition led by Yigael Yadin in 1960 and 1961 explored the caves in the area and found an abundance of artifacts from the era of Bar-Kokhba. Many of those discoveries may be viewed at the Shrine of the Book in Jerusalem.

MASADA

The Scriptures refer to many mountains of the Holy Land where important events took place. Yet one of the most frequently visited mountains in Israel is not mentioned in either the Old or New Testaments. That mountain is Masada (Hebrew for "stronghold"). Its very name stirs deep feelings of patriotism in the hearts of all Israelis. In 73 A.D. 960 Jewish men, women and children made a heroic stand at Masada against the Romans. Their persuasion that freedom was more precious than life itself has become a major symbol of modern Israel's commitment to the defense of liberty.

Herod the Great first acquired Masada during a fierce power-struggle in 46 B.C. Already fortified Masada became a temporary refuge for Herod's family when he was forced to flee from the Parthians and seek protection in Rome. Herod realized its importance, and began building a lavish palace-fortress on the twenty-acre summit in 30 B.C. Masada's ingenious construction and unique location made it nearly impregnable. A massive stone wall with thirty-eight defense towers was erected around the perimeter of the summit, giving it another dimension of protection against attack.

The northern slopes of Masada where Herod built his three-tiered palace.

Herod's complex atop Masada included two large palaces and several smaller ones. One palace erected in three tiers on the slopes of the north side served mainly for entertainment and leisure; the other larger palace which served as the prime residence was located on the western side.

Huge storehouses constructed near the northern palace held vast quantities of grain, food and beverages. A series of cisterns cut out of solid rock, with a combined capacity of 1,440,000 cubic feet, were used to store water. Where was the source for so much water in the middle of the desert? Two small wadis which pass to the north and south of Masada were dammed and aqueducts were built. Using the principle of gravity, water flowed freely halfway up Masada to a huge cistern. From there it was transported by donkeys to cisterns at the top of Masada. The path used to carry the water to the summit is still visible today. Enough water was collected and stored in the cisterns to allow the residents to grow gardens, fill Herod's swimming pool, supply their bath house, and still have an abundance for personal use.

At the outset of the First Jewish Revolt in 66 A.D., a number of Jewish zealots seized the fortress of Masada from the Romans. Just how they accomplished this feat is not known, but apparently the Romans were taken by surprise. The zealots then used Masada as a refuge for themselves and their families and as a base to launch attacks on Roman garrisons nearby.

In 70 A.D. Roman forces completely devastated Jerusalem and the surrounding countryside. Some of the Jewish survivors fled to Masada where they joined the last contingent of rebels still defying Rome. Atop Masada hundreds of people lived in the lavish palaces of King Herod. Concerned more with survival than refined living, however, the Jews partitioned their personal quarters as required. They built stone cook stoves on the beautiful mosaic tile floors, and took whatever other liberties the situation demanded. Herod's storehouses and cisterns provided above and beyond their needs. They rebuilt Masada's synagogue and constructed ritual baths (miqva'ot). This self-contained community of Jews became both an irritant and an embarrassment to the Romans.

In 72 A.D. Flavius Silva led a large Roman force to attack the Jewish rebels on Masada. Silva set up his headquarters at the base of

Masada's western side. He also constructed eight base camps and connected each with a siege wall. The ruins of Silva's camps may be seen today from the top of Masada.

Unable to remove the Jews by force because of the terrain and the defense structures, Silva set out to construct an earthen assault ramp against the western side of the mountain, from which his war machines and forces would attack. The ramp, constructed by Silva's soldiers, measured 225 yards in length and about the same in width at its broadest part. At the top of the assault ramp, he constructed a high siege tower plated with iron and equipped with catapults and battering ram. After months of effort the ramp was finally completed. Silva's battering ram began to hammer away at the outer defense wall. When it became apparent to the Jews that the wall was going to be breached, an inner wall of wood and earth was hastily constructed, likely with large timbers from the palaces. The inner wall was set ablaze by the Romans, though the fires nearly destroyed their own siege tower. Flavius Silva realized that the victory would soon be his. So did the Jews.

That night the men of Masada gathered around their leader Eleazar Ben Yair. It was obvious that their doom was sealed. They reasoned that they would all be killed at dawn and that likely their wives and children would also be killed or, even worse, made slaves and prostitutes of the Romans. Rather than becoming victims of the barbaric Romans, they preferred to die by their own hands. Thus, it was decided that each father would be required to put to death the members of his own family. Then ten specially chosen men would put the others to death.

Soon only ten men were left alive. They drew lots to see which one of them would kill the rest. The chosen one did his task quickly, for those still alive felt that every extra moment was an affront to those who had already died. Finally, the last man alive on Masada thrust his sword through his own body. It was Passover, 73 A.D.

In the morning light, the Romans entered Masada and discovered the bodies of 960 Jewish patriots. Death had come to them, not by the might of Roman warfare or ingenious Roman strategy, but by their own decision to die as free Jews rather than as Roman slaves. Two women and five children who had hidden in the caves of Masada came forth to tell their story to the Romans and to the world.

Cable car ascends to the top of Masada.

The first-century historian, Josephus, rendered a rather thorough account of this event in his *Jewish Wars*. Scholars have endeavored to piece together the incredible story of the Jews' last stand at Masada with Josephus' account and the archaeological evidence.

A few years ago, it was the practice of the Israeli Defense Forces to pledge recruits for their special units on the top of Masada where they took their oath of allegiance and affirmed, "Masada shall not fall again." These induction ceremonies now take place at the Western Wall.

An archaeological expedition under the leadership of Yigael Yadin was conducted at Masada between October 1963 and April 1965. While some earlier efforts had been made, Masada's secrets still waited to be discovered. Because of the dry desert air and the debris which covered everything, the archaeologists' discoveries were beyond their fondest expectations. The buildings described in the above accounts were unearthed, as well as many additional structures, revealing beautiful mosaic floors and other works of art. A number of human skeletons were found, some lying next to each other as described by the ancient historian, Josephus. Coins, clothing, scrolls, fragments of parchment, weapons and various personal effects were all there to reveal the truth about the 960 Jews' great struggle for freedom. Artifacts from Masada are now on display in Jerusalem.

One may reach the 1200 foot summit of Masada by climbing the "snake path" on its eastern side or by walking the less difficult path which incorporates the old Roman ramp on the western slopes. Not feeling inclined to either of those options, visitors may ascend and descend via a modern and very safe cable car. However, after arriving at the limits of the cable car, a considerable number of steps must still be climbed. The ground is uneven on the summit, making walking somewhat difficult. Because the sun can be unrelenting on Masada, visitors are cautioned to take proper precautions by wearing a head covering and by drinking plenty of water.

Signs atop Masada point out the various routes to follow for the tour; others identify sites of interest. A black line painted on the ruins shows how high the rubble was before the excavations were begun. Everything below the black line is in its original condition; everything above the line either jutted above the rubble or was reconstructed by the archaeologists.

ישראל

ISRAEL

Through Samaria
To Nazareth

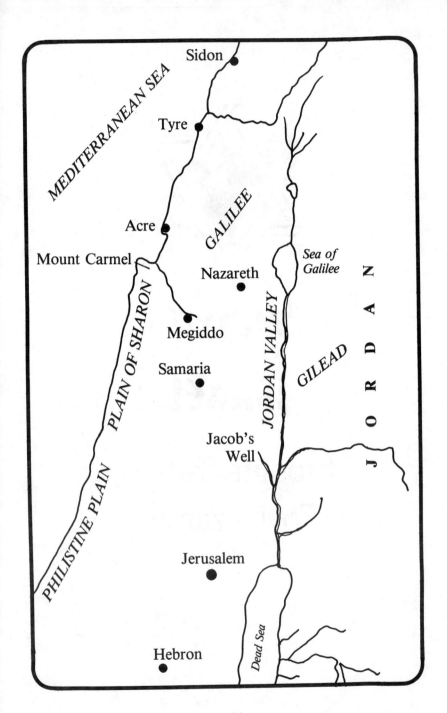

Through Samaria To Nazareth

THE REGION OF SAMARIA

After his death, King Solomon's kingdom was divided into two parts. The confederation of the northern tribes came to be called Israel, while the territories of Judah, Benjamin and Simeon were joined together to form the southern kingdom of Judah. Later, a portion of the northern kingdom became known as Samaria. It was bounded in the south by the road leading from Bethel to Jericho, in the east by the Jordan River, in the north by Mount Carmel and Mount Gilboa, and in the west by the Mediterranean Sea.

Most of the people were carried off into captivity when the Assyrians captured the northern kingdom in 722 B.C. Some Israelites remained, however, and were joined by foreigners who had been sent into the area as settlers by Assyria. Soon the cultures and religions of these peoples became blended. Following the Babylonian exile, the returning Jews looked upon their northern neighbors in Samaria with deep suspicion. The Jews had no time for the Samaritans by the New Testament age, believing them to be a corrupted people with a corrupted religion. They avoided passing through Samaria whenever possible, even if it added many miles to their journeys. For Jesus to make a Samaritan the *hero* in His parable of the Good Samaritan was very offensive to most Jews who heard it.

Unwilling and unwelcome to worship in Jerusalem, the Samaritans erected their own temple on Mount Gerizim. Many of the sacred events attributed to Mount Moriah in Scripture were transferred to Mount Gerizim by the Samaritans. They professed (and still do) that Abraham offered up Isaac on Mount Gerizim. Further, they believed Gerizim was the site of the Garden of Eden, the place where Moses

131

was permitted to view the Promised Land, the location of the altar built by Joshua, and the setting for many other biblical events.

A small remnant of Samaritans, numbering about 500 persons, survives today in two closely knit communities. One group lives at Nablus and the other at Holon, near Tel Aviv. The high priest, who is also the leader of the Samaritans, resides at Nablus. The Samaritans are very strict in their religious observances which resemble those of the Orthodox Jews, and they adhere exclusively to the Five Books of Moses.

SHECHEM

The modern Arab town of Nablus, situated between Mount Gerizim and Mount Ebal, is the site of ancient biblical Shechem. Jacob camped there with his family upon returning from Haran (Genesis 33:18). Jacob's sons, Simeon and Levi, killed the men of Shechem in revenge for the outrage committed against their sister, Dinah (Genesis 34). Shechem is also mentioned in Acts 7.

MOUNT GERIZIM AND MOUNT EBAL

These two important Old Testament mountains tower over central Samaria. They stand side by side with the town of Nablus (Shechem) between them. Gerizim is 2890 feet above sea level and Ebal rises 3084 feet.

Gerizim is the most sacred place of the Samaritan religion. Each year they celebrate the Passover on its summmit. The Lord instructed the children of Israel to gather at Gerizim and Ebal after they had entered the Promised Land. There they were to hear the blessings of God for obedience to His law and the curses of God for disobedience (Deut. 11:29). Accordingly, Joshua assembled the people before Mount Gerizim and Mount Ebal.

Half of the people stood in front of Mount Gerizim and half of them in front of Mount Ebal, as Moses the servant of the Lord had formerly commanded when he gave instructions to bless the people of Israel. Afterward, Joshua read all the words of the law the blessings and the curses- just as it is written in the

Book of the Law. There was not a word of all that Moses had commanded that Joshua did not read to the whole assembly of Israel, including the women and children, and the aliens who lived among them

(Joshua 8:33–35).

JACOB'S WELL

A short distance from the eastern base of Mount Gerizim is Jacob's Well, one of the oldest and most authentic sites in the Holy Land. Dug by the patriarch Jacob himself, according to tradition, it is located on property owned by the Greek Orthodox Church. The well which still functions today is approximately 115 feet deep. Visitors are welcome to drink the cool, refreshing water.

Access to the well itself is below ground in a little chapel tended by the Orthodox priests. Many years ago an attempt was made to build a church over the site, but it has never been completed. The unfinished structure stands on the ruins of a fourth-century church and a Crusader church.

Jesus met a woman of Samaria at Jacob's Well when she came to draw water in the middle of the day. This unusual encounter gave Him the opportunity to minister to the Samaritans for several days, much to the surprise of His disciples (John 4: 1-42). Philip experienced a readiness on the part of the Samaritans to receive the Gospel (Acts 8:4–8), and Peter was doing follow-up work in Samaria when he encountered Simon the sorcerer (Acts 8:9–25).

THE CITY OF SAMARIA

Samaria, the capital of the northern kingdom of Israel, was founded by King Omri in 876 B.C. (1 Kings 16:24). His son, Ahab, who lived in Samaria with his notorious wife, Jezebel, completed the city's construction in elaborate fashion. Several of the buildings were adorned with ivory. The Assyrians destroyed the city in 722 B.C.

Herod the Great rebuilt Samaria in 25 B.C. and named it Sabaste, the name used by the Arab residents living there today. Outstanding excavations of the old city of Sabaste in this century revealed column-lined streets, a Roman theater, a temple to Augustus Caesar, a stadium and a Roman basilica. The ruins from ancient Samaria were also uncovered, including portions of Omri's palace with over 500 unique pieces of ivory which had decorated the palace and its furniture. The prophet Amos denounced the leadership of Israel for their utter disregard of the poor:

> Woe to you who are complacent in Zion, and to you who feel secure on Mount Samaria . . . You lie on beds inlaid with ivory and lounge on your couches
>
> *(Amos 6:1 and 4).*

MOUNT GILBOA

Rising from the Plain of Esdraelon (Jezreel), Mount Gilboa stands only 1759 feet above sea level. The mountain is eleven miles long and approximately five miles wide, and is chiefly remembered as the scene of the great battle between Israel and the Philistines.

"How the mighty have fallen!" lamented King David upon hearing the news that Saul and his sons had died in battle at Mount Gilboa. "Tell it not in Gath, proclaim it not in the streets of Ashkelon," he pleaded, "lest the daughters of the Philistines be glad, lest the daughters of the uncircumcised rejoice." In David's great sorrow he cursed Gilboa. (2 Samuel 1:17–27).

MOUNT TABOR

Mount Tabor is one of the most picturesque mountains in Israel. Although only 1929 feet above sea level, its elevation from the plains which surround the base makes it appear much larger. A narrow road winds precariously to its rounded top.

More impressive than the buildings on its summit is the view of the surrounding countryside. On a clear day it is possible to see the Horns of Hattin where Saladin defeated the Crusaders on July 4, 1187, as well as the snow-capped peaks of Mount Hermon. There is also a marvelous view of the Valley of Jezreel, the Bet Shean Valley and the Carmel range.

Mount Tabor is mentioned several times in the Bible. Deborah instructed Barak to gather his forces there to fight against the king of

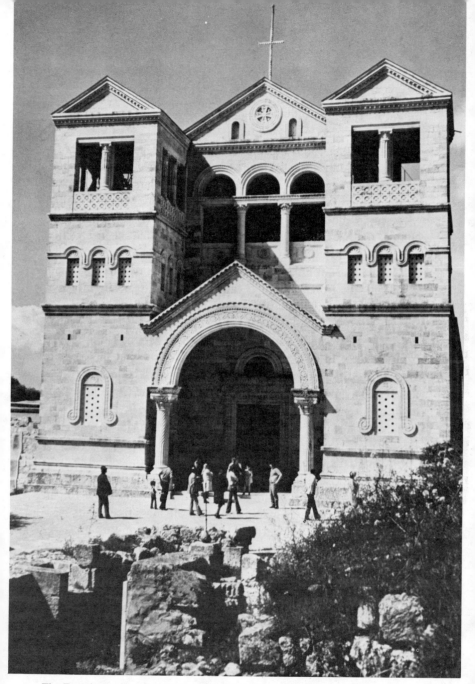

The Franciscan Church at Mount Tabor, traditional site of the transfiguration of Christ.

Hazor. In that battle, the Canaanites became bogged down in the mire of the rain-soaked Valley of Jezreel, and the army of Deborah and Barak rushed to destroy them in an area very near Megiddo (Judges 4–5). Other Old Testament references include: Hosea 5:1, and Jeremiah 46:18.

A tradition that Tabor was the setting for the transfiguration of Jesus became widely accepted in the Roman Church during the Byzantine period. Other ancient and some modern scholars have contended that the scene of the transfiguration is more likely Mount Hermon. A Byzantine church was constructed on Mount Tabor in the fourth century. A Crusader edifice constructed on the same site around 1100 was destroyed just a few years later, but another Crusader building replaced it. The Greek Orthodox who maintain a presence on Mount Tabor built their church on the site of the Crusader church in 1911.

The Orthodox and Roman areas on Tabor are walled off from each other. Separate roads lead to their respective properties. The Roman Catholics constructed a rather large church on Mount Tabor in 1924 with two small chapels, one dedicated to Moses and the other to Elijah. In addition, there is a Franciscan hospice and monastery, as well as a convent. On the Greek compound are the Church of Saint Elijah and a monastery. The Cave of Melchizedek is also in the Greek section. Supposedly it was at this cave that Melchizedek met Abraham and received tithes from him (Genesis 14:17–20).

For Christians, the primary focus of Mount Tabor is the transfiguration of Jesus (Luke 9:28–36). On this or another "high mountain," Jesus was transfigured in glory and talked with Moses and Elijah.

While Catholics may worship and celebrate mass freely in the Roman church, Protestant Christians are seldom permitted the same privilege. Instead, they must use the grounds surrounding the church, which, as a general rule, is actually much preferred. It is sad, however, that so much of the Protestant community is forbidden to worship in churches located on various sacred sites throughout the Holy Land. Strictly speaking, the Roman and Orthodox Church bodies which occupy the sites are *stewards and caretakers* and not the owners. They are most unfair to deny Protestant Christians their *right to worship* at these various places.

MEGIDDO

The ruins of the ancient fortress-city of Megiddo were discovered on the western side of the Valley of Jezreel. Megiddo overlooks the Plain of Armageddon, one of the world's oldest and most renowned battlefields. Built near a narrow pass and the intersection of two major highways, Megiddo became a most strategic fortress. One highway led from Megiddo in a northwesterly direction to Acre and beyond. This highway branched off from the main road which continued eastward from Megiddo to the Jordan Valley and west through a narrow pass to the Plain of Sharon.

A two-year archaeological expedition was begun at Megiddo in 1903 by a group of Germans. From 1925 until 1939, archaeologists from the University of Chicago worked at Megiddo in one of the most extensive expeditions ever conducted in the Middle East. They discovered that the tell of Megiddo contained the ruins of twenty cities built one on top of the other over many centuries. The first city built on bedrock dated to around 3500 B.C., while the twentieth city located seventy feet above the first dated to about 450 B.C.

The primary ruins uncovered at Megiddo date to the time of Omri and Ahab. Discoveries included stables built to accommodate as many as 500 horses. Also uncovered at Megiddo are the ruins of a main gate, palaces, a huge grain silo, a Canaanite altar, and a unique water system.

Like Gihon at Jerusalem, the water supply at Megiddo was located outside the walls, making the fortress extremely vulnerable. Ahab constructed a shaft cut out of solid rock from the top of Megiddo to a spring outside the fortress. The impressive tunnel which is nearly 200 feet long may be approached today by descending 183 steps, exiting on the other side by climbing only 80 steps.

Megiddo is mentioned often in the Old Testament, usually in connection with battles fought on the plains below. Even in post-biblical times the area was the scene of many military engagements. Joshua defeated the king of Megiddo and made the fortress a possession of the tribe of Manasseh (Joshua 12:21), but it was not fully in Israel's control until the time of David. Deborah and Barak won a great victory over the Canaanite king, Sisera, in the Valley of Megiddo (Judges 4). King Ahaziah died at Megiddo after being wounded by

Jehu (2 Kings 23:29). The New Testament reveals that the last battle on earth will be fought at Armageddon (Revelation 16:16).

The museum at Megiddo displays various artifacts found on the site, as well as an interesting model of the fortress as it appeared in the days of Omri and Ahab. For years it was believed that many of the ruins at Megiddo were from the Solomonic period, but scholars now claim they are from the later period of the northern kingdom.

NAZARETH

"Can anything good come out of Nazareth?" inquired Nathanael when he first learned of Jesus (John 1:46). Nathanael's attitude towards Nazareth is reflected in the fact that not once is the city mentioned in the Old Testament. Nazareth's only claim to fame was through the miracle-working son of Mary and Joseph who resided there. While the New Testament is largely silent regarding Jesus' first thirty years, most scholars believe that they were lived in Nazareth, except for the brief period immediately following Jesus' birth when Joseph took his young family into exile in Egypt. It is presumed that Jesus worked with His father in the carpenter shop and attended synagogue school, as was the custom of Jewish boys at that time. Since the New Testament makes no further mention of Joseph after Jesus reached the age of twelve, it is assumed that Joseph died prior to the time that Jesus began His public ministry.

Today Nazareth stands on the slopes of Lower Galilee, 1230 feet above sea level. From Nazareth one has a commanding view of the Valley of Esdraelon (Jezreel), one of Israel's most beautiful and fertile valleys. The streets and alleys of Nazareth wind about the hills with their closely quartered homes and churches. The majority of her 45,000 inhabitants are Christian Arabs of five different denominations, and the balance of the Arab population is Moslem.

A large and growing Jewish settlement, numbering 27,000, is located on the upper slopes of Nazareth. These Jews have brought several large industries to the city, greatly improving the economic welfare of the local Arab community. The city has been a part of Israel since its capture on July 16, 1948. For years the Jews and Arabs of Nazareth have lived together peacefully, but that relationship has been recently shaken by the Palestinian uprisings.

The Roman Catholic Church of the Annunciation in Nazareth, built over the traditional home of the Virgin Mary.

As a predominantly Christian city and the boyhood home of Jesus, Nazareth is a city of churches. Two of her oldest and most important churches claim to be built on the site of the annunciation.

THE ROMAN CATHOLIC CHURCH OF THE ANNUNCIATION

The Roman Catholics chose to erect their Church of the Annunciation over the traditional home of Mary. It is surely the largest and one of the most beautiful churches in the Middle East. The Church was dedicated in 1964 by Pope Paul VI, but was not completed until 1969. Built on two levels, the centerpiece for both is a huge dome shaped like an inverted lily. Beneath the dome on the lower level are the ruins of a first-century home which, according to Roman Catholic tradition, was the home of Mary and the place of the annunciation. A small chapel directly beneath the dome faces the entrance to the ancient house.

The upper level is the main sanctuary. Its walls are adorned with mosaics that were given by people in various nations of the world. Each mosaic portrays the mother of Jesus in one theme or another. Above the main altar a mural depicts "Christ standing with Peter on Mount Zion, and Mary sitting in the background praying for her children who are streaming in from all sides for the eternal feast."

Just how far back in history this site has been venerated is unclear. It is certain that a Byzantine church and later a Crusader church were constructed here. Remnants of both churches may be viewed in and around the present structure.

A short distance from the Church of the Annunciation is the Church of St. Joseph, erected above the alleged residence of Mary and Joseph and over Joseph's carpenter shop. There is little to authenticate this tradition, however. There is strong evidence that an ancient church once stood on this same site and dated to the second or third century. The present church was built in 1914.

THE SYNAGOGUE CHURCH

Nearby is the Greek Synagogue Church, so named because it stands on the traditional site of a first-century synagogue which some believe Jesus attended as a boy and where He later read from the scroll of Isaiah, chapter sixty-one (Luke 4:16-21). It was from that synagogue that the crowd led Jesus to the brow of the hill and attempted to throw Him off (Luke 4:22–30). Frankly, there is not sufficient evidence to authenticate the Synagogue Church, but it is valuable for recalling these events from the life of Jesus.

One hill near Nazareth is presented as the Mount of Precipitation where the crowd attempted to push Jesus to His death, but certain identification is impossible. The location of Nazareth in Lower Galilee among so many steep hills helps one to visualize this biblical event.

THE GREEK ORTHODOX CHURCH OF THE ANNUNCIATION

The Greek Orthodox Church of the Annunciation (Saint Gabriel's) also claims to be erected over the site of the annunciation. Inside the Greek Church is a spring called Mary's Well. Some ancient traditions claim that Gabriel appeared to Mary as she went to draw water (Luke 1:26–38). While the present church building is of late construction, it is known that a Crusader church was located on the site, and possibly a Byzantine church also.

Many visitors and tour groups are hurried through Nazareth without adequate time to ponder its spiritual significance. This is quite unfortunate, because they miss not only its beautiful and historic churches but also the opportunity to reflect on the scenes so precious to Jesus as a child. How meaningful it is to stand on Nazareth's heights and meditate on the Scriptures as they relate to Jesus.

Then he went down to Nazareth with them and was obedient to them. But his mother treasured all these things in her heart. And Jesus grew in wisdom and stature, and in favor with God and men

(Luke 2:51-52).

CANA

Only a few miles from Nazareth on the road to Tiberias is the little Arab village known as Kefar Kanna. It was here that Jesus performed His first miracle by turning the water into wine (John 2:1-11).

Jesus was in Cana when a nobleman from Capernaum approached Him and requested that He return with him to heal his son. Assured that his son would be healed, the man went home believing what Jesus told him (John 4:46–50). Cana was also the home of Nathanael (John 21:2).

Two churches of significance are located in Cana, one Roman Catholic, the other Greek Orthodox. The present Roman Catholic structure is built on the ruins of a fourth-century church and claims to be located on the site where Jesus turned the water into wine. The Greek Church claims to have the water jar in which the miracle was performed.

ישראל

ISRAEL

Around The Sea
Of Galilee

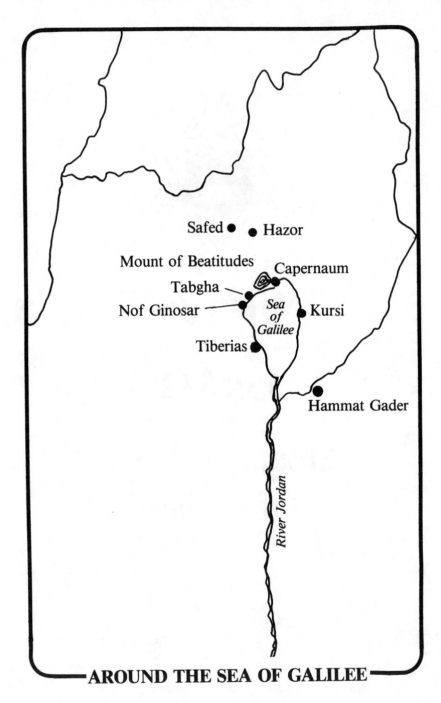

Safed ●   ● Hazor

Mount of Beatitudes
Tabgha
Nof Ginosar

Capernaum

*Sea
of
Galilee*

Kursi

Tiberias ●

Hammat Gader

River Jordan

AROUND THE SEA OF GALILEE

Around The Sea Of Galilee

THE SEA OF GALILEE - Lake Gennesaret

The Sea of Galilee's pastoral setting forever lingers in the memory once you have seen it. Because so many sites in the Holy Land have been covered over by churches and shrines, it is refreshing to see an entire area appearing much as it did in the days of the Bible. For the most part, the countryside is still resplendent in its natural beauty. One can quickly appreciate why the Lord spent so much time along its tranquil shores. The Golan Heights rise above the lake's eastern shore, and in the distant north you can often make out the peaks of Mount Hermon. On the western side, the fertile hills roll gently to the shore. Whether in the soft light of sunrise, in the full blaze of day, or at the glow of sundown, the Sea of Galilee wondrously declares the glory of God.

The Jordan River originates in the foothills of Mount Hermon, then flows into the northern side of Galilee and out again at its southern end. Finally it completes its winding flow at the Dead Sea. The Jordan River is the principal source of water for the Sea of Galilee. Known in the Old Testament as Kinnereth and in the New Testament as Lake Gennesaret, the Sea of Galilee lies 688 feet below sea level. It is thirteen miles long, seven miles wide, and at its deepest point measures 144 feet.

Numerous fishing boats may be seen moving on the waters or docked along the shores, for the lake still has an abundance of fish as it did in Bible times. There are twenty-two known species of fish in Lake Gennesaret, including the mousht (St. Peter's fish), so named because of the fish which Peter caught with the coin in its mouth (Matthew 17:24–27). Walking along the shore one day Jesus summoned Peter, Andrew, James and John, all fishermen, to follow

145

Him and become "fishers of men" (Mark 1:16-20). Luke tells how Jesus assisted His friends to catch so many fish that their boat began to sink (Luke 5:4-7).

Because of its size and location below sea level, as well as its nearness to high mountains and hills, significant temperature changes and strong winds sometimes produce sudden and violent storms. Such a storm caused the disciples to believe that they were about to perish, even though Jesus was sleeping in their boat. With the simple command, "Peace be still," Jesus calmed the angry waves as well as the anxious hearts of His disciples (Mark 4:36-41). Many a storm-tossed heart will affirm that Jesus is able to perform that miracle today. On another occasion, Jesus walked upon the waters of Galilee (Matthew 14:22-33).

Of the thirty-three specific healing miracles which are recorded in the New Testament, Jesus performed ten of them in the area of Galilee. The Bible also records scenes where many persons were healed by Jesus in the course of His ministry in Galilee, but details are not given. It is interesting to note that there were several therapeutic hot springs near Tiberias in Bible times. These were especially popular with the Romans. The hot springs might explain why so many sick people sought out Jesus in the Galilee area.

At the time of Christ, the region around Galilee was densely populated. One of the area's most important towns was Capernaum where Jesus made His headquarters. Other towns around Galilee which Jesus visited include: Bethsaida, Chorazin, Magdala and Gergesa. Three of these cities (Chorazin, Bethsaida and Capernaum) were condemned by Jesus because of their great unbelief.

Following the destruction of Jerusalem, Galilee became the spiritual center of Jewish life. Many renowned Jewish leaders lived, wrote, and taught in the area. During the Byzantine era and the Crusader period, Christianity also flourished in the region of Galilee.

TIBERIAS

Tiberias is mentioned only once in the New Testament. Built in 22 A.D. by Herod Antipas, son of Herod the Great, the city was not frequently visited by Jews during the time of Christ. The city was

The Sea of Galilee.

unholy to them, not only because it was Herod's capital, but especially because it had been built over an ancient cemetery.

The city was named in honor of Emperor Tiberias who was ruling in Rome at the time. Likely the location attracted Herod because of the hot mineral springs and pleasing climate. In keeping with the times, Herod enclosed the city with defensive walls.

After the fall of Jerusalem in 70 A.D., Tiberias became an important center of Jewish life, serving as the seat of the Sanhedrin. The Jewish Mishnah (a collection of traditional Jewish law) was developed here in the second century. Also, in the fourth century, the Talmud (the Mishnah with commentary) was developed in Tiberias. Maimonides, the famous Jewish physician and philosopher who died in 1204, is buried in this city. He is considered a forerunner of modern medicine. Another notable from Tiberias, Rabbi Akiva, who once called Bar-Kokhba the "Messiah," is also buried here.

After the Crusaders captured the city in 1099, they strengthened its walls and fortifications, portions of which still stand today. The Crusaders used the city as their capital of the northern region. But Tiberias fell to Saladin in 1187 when the Crusaders lost a crucial battle at the Horns of Hattin, not far from the city. Saladin destroyed Tiberias, and it was not rebuilt until the sixteenth century. In 1837 it was partially destroyed by an earthquake. The restored city was captured by the British in 1918 and by the Israelis in 1948.

Today Tiberias is a growing Jewish city full of hotels and restaurants. Its hot mineral baths are still a major attraction, as well as the lake itself. Being 680 feet below sea level, Tiberias is especially enjoyable during the winter months.

TABGHA

North of Tiberias and also on the western side of the Sea of Galilee is Tabgha, the traditional site where Jesus fed the 5,000 with five loaves and two fish (Mark 6:35–44). Excavations here uncovered the remains of a mosaic floor from a fifth-century church appropriately called The Church of the Multiplication of the Loaves and Fishes. A new church by the same name, erected by the Benedictines in 1982, is styled in a manner similar to the original fifth-century church. The new structure incorporates the ancient fifth-century

A boat ride on the Sea of Galilee offers a unique vista of the area, as well as an inspirational scene for worship.

floor, one of the most beautiful mosaic floors ever discovered in Israel. On the floor in front of the altar is a mosaic of the loaves and fishes. Beneath the altar is a stone which some maintain served as the table for the blessing of the loaves and fishes.

THE CHURCH OF THE PRIMACY OF PETER

A short distance from Tabgha is another site which recalls a post-resurrection appearance of Jesus, the reinstatement of Peter following his three-fold denial (John 21:15-19). On the site is a small chapel erected by the Franciscans in 1934. Inside the chapel are the ruins of a fourth-century church. In front of the chapel's altar is a flat rock which was incorporated in the ancient church and believed to be the table on which the Lord prepared breakfast for the disciples (John 21:1-14). While no one may be certain concerning the location of these two events in the life of Christ, it is known that they occurred in the general area. The fact that this site and several others nearby have been venerated as early as the fourth century does give it some degree of plausibility.

THE MOUNT OF BEATITUDES

A small hill to the west of Tabgha has been known for centuries as the Mount of Beatitudes. Originally a small church dating to the fourth century stood on the site. Though it was destroyed in the seventh century, the church was not replaced until 1937 when the Italian dictator Mussolini donated the required funds for the construction of a new church further up the hill. The church is octagonal in shape, commemorating the eight beatitudes. Glass on all sides allows worshippers to see the beautiful scenery below. On a clear day, the views of Lake Gennesaret are especially spectacular. The church is cared for by the Italian Franciscan Sisters whose convent is on the property.

CAPERNAUM

One of the highlights of a visit to the Sea of Galilee is Capernaum, the center of Jesus' ministry in the area. The Scriptures refer to it as

The Church on the Mount of Beatitudes.

151

"his own city" (Matthew 9:1). In New Testament times, Capernaum's population was likely between ten and fifteen thousand.

Extinct for centuries, the ruins of Capernaum have been uncovered in this century by the Franciscans who acquired the property in 1894. Their most important discovery so far is a synagogue dating to the fourth century and built upon the foundations of a first-century synagogue. The older ruins are likely remnants of the same synagogue which was erected through the generosity of a Roman soldier (Luke 7). It was here that Jesus taught, and also healed the man possessed with an unclean spirit (Mark 1:21–28).

While attempting to rebuild the fourth-century synagogue, the priest in charge, Father Orfali, was killed in an automobile accident. Among the ruins of the synagogue stands a column with an inscription in Orfali's memory. Following the priest's untimely death, the work of restoring the synagogue was halted as some remembered the condemnation which Jesus had placed on Capernaum (Matthew 11:23). Another ancient column which was found among the ruins of the synagogue has an inscription which reads: "Alphaeus, son of Zebedee, son of John, made this column, on him be blessing."

Many events of Jesus' ministry in Capernaum are preserved in the Gospels. Mark tells of Jesus entering the home of Peter and Andrew and healing Peter's mother-in-law of a fever (Mark 1:29–31). The Franciscans believe that they have uncovered the home of Peter beneath the ruins of a fifth- century octagonal church. The Franciscans are now attempting to construct another church on the site, but they have been stopped, for the time being, by the Israeli Department of Antiquities.

It was in Capernaum that Jesus called Levi (Matthew) to leave his tax collecting and follow Him. Later Jesus went to supper at Levi's home, creating no small stir among His critics (Mark 2:13-17).

Other incidents of Jesus' ministry in Capernaum include: the healing of Jarius' daughter (Matthew 9:18), the centurion's servant (Matthew 8:5-13), the man brought by his friends and lowered to Jesus through the roof (Mark 2:1-5), and the Roman official's son (John 4:46–53).

KURSI

The ruins of a Byzantine monastery stand at the base of a steep hill where tradition maintains that Jesus cast out demons from a man and sent them into a herd of swine. Immediately the swine ran headlong into the Sea of Galilee and drowned (Luke 8:26–39).

The ancient monastic compound is surrounded by walls with a rather large church in the center. Portions of a mosaic tile floor still remain, as well as a large olive press.

HAMMAT GADER

Hammat Gader was once one of the most beautiful Roman baths in the world and second largest in the entire empire. Excavations made since 1979 have revealed six different pools with their connecting halls and walkways. One colonnade measures twenty-five feet high. The hot springs of Hammat Gader still function and are operated by Israel as part of a national park system. These Roman ruins are located five miles southeast of the Sea of Galilee at the foot of the Golan Heights.

THE ANCIENT BOAT

During an extreme dry spell in 1986, two members of the Nof Ginosar Kibbutz happened upon an ancient boat jutting out of the receded waters of the Sea of Galilee. Embedded in mud which preserved the ancient craft, the boat was laboriously uncovered and moved to a temporary location near the Yigal Allon Center on Kibbutz Ginosar. Experts have dated the boat from first century B.C. to first century A.D. Scholars now confirm that this is a fishing boat such as was used in New Testament times. The boat measures 26.6 feet long, 7.6 feet wide and 4.6 high. Presently the ancient vessel is immersed in a special preservative. Eventually it will be placed in a chemical solution of synthetic wax for seven years, during which time the wax will replace the water in the wood.

The synagogue in Capernaum.

SAFED (ZEFAT)

One of the most interesting towns in Israel today is Safed (Zefat in Hebrew), a Jewish city nestled 2800 feet above sea level in the Galilean hills. Because Safed is clearly visible from the Sea of Galilee area, some believe that Jesus was referring to Safed when He spoke of "the city on a hill which cannot be hidden" (Matthew 5:14). Zefat literally means "place of outlook." The city offers a commanding view of the surrounding region from its heights, over 3400 feet above the Sea of Galilee. In ancient times a signal announcing the new moon was passed from the Mount of Olives to other high mountains throughout the land. The last signal was relayed to Upper Galilee from Zefat.

Safed's altitude and cool breezes make it an ideal summer resort. One of its modern distinctives is an artists' colony where a considerable number of painters, sculptors, poets and writers reside. Along its hilly and crooked streets, shops offer various works of art by these locals.

Safed was a Crusader city until it was captured by the Arabs in 1187, who used it as their headquarters for controlling Upper Galilee. In the sixteenth century it became an important center of Jewish learning. A group of Jews known as the Cabbalists resided there and were famous for their mystic studies. Cabbalist studies are still common in Safed. In 1607 there were supposedly over 300 rabbis, 18 rabbinical colleges and 21 synagogues in Safed. The first printing press in the Middle East was operated in Safed, printing a book in Hebrew for the first time in 1561.

The city has experienced some drastic population changes in more recent history. A devastating earthquake destroyed the city in 1837, killing over 4,000 people. In 1948 it was inhabited by 12,000 Arabs and only 1700 Jews. On May 11, 1948, Safed was captured by the Israelis, and the entire Arab community fled and never returned.

HAZOR

Like Megiddo in Lower Galilee, Hazor in Upper Galilee was an ancient fortress-city located along an important highway. Hazor was built on two levels. The upper city was approximately 25 acres in size, while the lower city was 150 acres. Although ruins from ancient civilizations have been unearthed at Hazor, the city is not mentioned in the Bible until its conquest and destruction by Joshua. At the time of Joshua, it was the most important city in that region. Jabin, king of Hazor, joined several other kings to fight against Israel, but Joshua prevailed and burned Hazor to the ground (Joshua 11).

Deborah and Barak successfully fought against Jabin, king of Hazor, and his general, Sisera, several decades later at Megiddo. Because the king's name in Judges 4 is the same as the king killed by Joshua (Joshua 11), some critics maintain that these are two differing accounts of the same battle. However, the archaeological evidence clearly reveals that after Joshua destroyed Hazor, new settlements were made in the upper city. It was the settlement in the upper city which was destroyed in the time of the Judges.

Hazor was enlarged and rebuilt by Solomon. Later it was strengthened and enlarged by Omri and Ahab because of its strategic importance. Hazor's final destruction came in 732 B.C. at the hands of the Assyrians.

The mound of Hazor was first examined in 1928, but it was not fully excavated until 1955-1958 by Yigael Yadin. Significant ruins from the time of Solomon were uncovered, together with extensive ruins from the time of Omri/Ahab. The excavations also revealed that the city gates and the water shaft resembled the ones at Megiddo.

ישראל

ISRAEL

Along The Coast

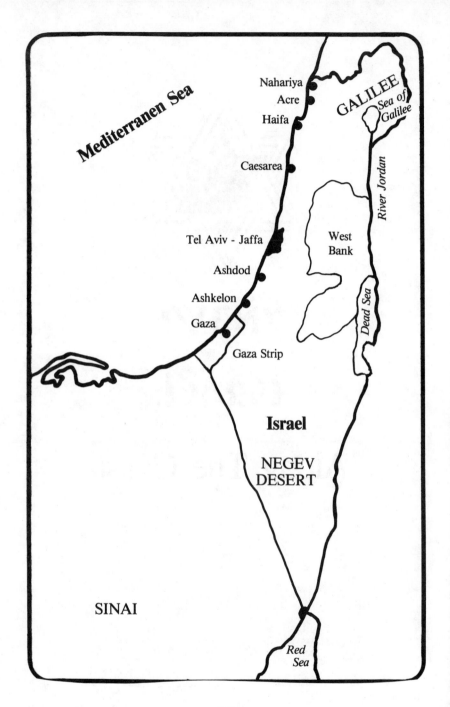

Along The Coast

THE GAZA STRIP

One of the most densely populated regions of the world is the Gaza Strip, at the extreme southwestern corner of Israel. More than 650,000 Arabs are crowded into one area which is only twenty-five miles long and averages four to eight miles wide. Nearly 200,000 residents live in refugee camps. Under Israeli control since 1967, the Gaza Strip has become Israel's chief trouble spot in the occupied territories. Since November 1987, the Arabs of Gaza and the West Bank have openly revolted against Israeli occupation.

The Gaza Strip was part of the British Mandate until 1948. When the British relinquished control, Gaza was occupied by Egypt as her army invaded Israel. Interestingly, in all the years that Egypt held the Gaza Strip, they never tried to annex it as Jordan had done with the West Bank and East Jerusalem. Israel had brief control of the area in 1956 following the Sinai War, but withdrew when international assurances were given that Egypt would not be permitted to use the region as a military base for attacks on Israel. Those assurances were honored until United Nations' troops stationed in the Gaza Strip following the 1956 Sinai War were ordered out just prior to the Six Day War by Egypt's President Nasser. But, when the last confrontation came in 1967, the Gaza Strip was captured by Israel on the fourth day of the war.

For the most part, the Gaza Strip is an economically depressed area. Unemployment is still high, even though a considerable number of Gaza's residents work in Israel. Except for some citrus farming, there is little local industry. Also, there is an acute shortage of doctors and hospitals.

Living conditions in the Gaza Strip have greatly deteriorated since the 1987-1988 uprising. It is estimated that 1,100,000 Arabs will be living there by the year 2000, over half under age 14. Israel made a commitment in the Camp David Accords to give the residents of the Gaza Strip self-rule. With the potential of more than a million hostile people living at the edge of the nation's major population centers, a solution suitable to both Jews and Arabs must be found quickly.

GAZA CITY

The modern city of Gaza, located two miles from the Mediterranean Sea and thirteen miles south of Ashkelon, stands on ruins which date to the Egyptian pharaohs, making it one of the oldest cities in the world.

Gaza was one of five important Philistine cities mentioned in the Old Testament. According to the Scriptures, Samson pulled up the gates of the city "bar and all and carried them to the top of the hill that is before Hebron" (Judges 16:3). After Delilah had Samson's hair cut, he was imprisoned and ultimately killed at Gaza (Judges 16). The prophets Amos and Zephaniah strongly denounced Gaza for treachery against Israel (Amos 1:7 and Zephaniah 2:4).

The city has seen many conquerors come and go. Napoleon camped at Gaza in 1799 when he unsuccessfully endeavored to capture the Holy Land from the Turks. The British lost over 10,000 lives when they seized control of Gaza from the Turks during World War I. Egypt used the city as a military base from 1948 to 1967, except for the brief period of Israeli occupation in 1956.

ASHKELON

The ruins of ancient Ashkelon, excavated in 1921, have been incorporated into a national park operated by the State of Israel. Located midway between Ashdod and the Gaza Strip, Ashkelon has a long and bloody history. Its conquerors include Ramses II of Egypt in the thirteenth century B.C., Tiglathpileser III of Assyria in 734 B.C., Sennacherib of Assyria in 701 B.C., Nebuchadnezzar of Babylon in 604 B.C., as well as a parade of Greek, Roman, Crusader and Arab armies.

The Crusaders controlled the city from 1153 to 1247, except for a few years when it was in the hands of Saladin. The city's name was changed to Ascalon by the Crusaders. The Moslems destroyed it in 1270.

Ashkelon is mentioned in the Old Testament as one of the five chief Philistine cities which were continually warring against Israel. King Saul was fighting the Philistines when he was mortally wounded and fell on his own sword at Mount Gilboa (1 Samuel 31). Upon hearing the news of Saul's death, David, in a lament, pleaded that the news not be told in the streets of Ashkelon (2 Samuel 1:20). To pay those who answered his riddle, Samson went to Ashkelon where he killed thirty men and took their festal garments (Judges 14:19).

Herod the Great was born in Ashkelon in 73 B.C., and his sister Salome resided there. He beautified the city streets and erected elaborate buildings. Philistine, Roman and Crusader ruins have all been excavated at Ashkelon.

A short distance from ancient Ashkelon is the modern town, developed since 1950 with the aid of South African Jewry. It is a lovely seaside-resort community with quality hotels and restaurants. At the entrance of the town is a memorial to the prophet Zephaniah with the following words of his prophecy:

> The sea coast shall become the possession of the remnant of the house of Judah, on which they shall pasture, and in the houses of Ashkelon they shall lie down at evening. For the Lord their God will be mindful of them and restore their fortunes (2:6–7).

ASHDOD

The ruins of ancient Ashdod, a Canaanite city founded in the sixteenth century B.C., were discovered eighteen miles south of Tel Aviv. Though assigned to the tribe of Judah (Joshua 15:46), the city remained in the control of the Philistines. It was one of five important Philistine cities mentioned in the Old Testament.

The most significant biblical reference to Ashdod concerns the capture of the Ark of the Covenant by the Philistines who placed it in their Temple of Dagon. The intent of the Philistines was to humiliate Israel by keeping the Ark in their possession, but its presence caused them no end of problems. Finally, in utter desperation, they sent it back (1 Samuel 5 and 6).

Ashdod is mentioned twenty-one times in the Old Testament, often in strong words of denunciation by the prophets, both before and after the Babylonian exile (Jeremiah 25:20; Amos 1:8; Zephaniah 2:4; and Zechariah 9:6). Nehemiah became extremely angry when he discovered that children born to Jews who had married women from Ashdod could not speak the Jewish language (Nehemiah 13:23–24). Another scriptural reference to Ashdod relates to its capture by King Uzziah (2 Chronicles 26:6).

When the Greeks controlled Ashdod, they named it Azotus. It is called by that name in Acts 8:40. Azotus was captured by the Maccabees and by Pompey who rebuilt the city. When Ashdod was excavated between 1962 and 1965, twenty different levels of the ancient city were discovered.

There is a modern city of Ashdod today. Founded in 1957, it is located four miles north of the ancient ruins. Its newly constructed deep-water harbor has greatly spurred the growth and economy of the area. Over half of the nation's cargoes are handled through this port. Large apartment and office buildings now stand where only sand dunes existed a few years ago. One of the city's most impressive structures is its new civic center. Many large industrial plants have been established in Ashdod.

JAFFA

Though now a part of Tel Aviv, Jaffa is a city whose history dates to the Canaanite period. Perhaps being the only seaport between Egypt and Acre in ancient times, it was most important to those who wanted to control the region. Thus, Jaffa has been ruled by many masters through the centuries, from Thutmose III of Egypt in 1468 B.C. to the Israeli conquest in 1948.

Jaffa (Yafo in Hebrew) was originally assigned to the tribe of Dan. However, it never became a part of Israel until captured from the Philistines by King David, who made it the seaport for Jerusalem. Hiram, king of Tyre, sent the famous cedars of Lebanon through the port of Jaffa for the construction of Solomon's Temple (2 Chronicles

The city of Joppa.

2:16). Seeking to escape the Lord's assignment in Ninevah, Jonah set sail from Jaffa for Tarshish, only to end up as an undigestible meal for a large fish (Jonah 1:17).

When Alexander the Great conquered the region, the city was re-named Joppa, as it was known in the New Testament. The apostle Peter was summoned to Joppa from nearby Lydda when the faithful woman, Tabitha (Dorcas), became ill and died. Through the power of prayer, Peter brought her to life again (Acts 9:36–41). While Peter was residing in Joppa at the house of Simon the tanner, he saw a puzzling vision of many unclean animals which he was commanded to kill and eat. The meaning of his vision became clearer a short time later when messengers sent by Cornelius of Caesarea arrived in Joppa (Acts 9:43-10:48).

Jaffa served as the main port-of-entry to the Holy Land throughout much of the Turkish period. According to the journals of some pilgrims, the experience was not always pleasant. John W. Dullas wrote of his adventures in 1881:

> The landing at Joppa has a bad name, and deservedly. Properly speaking, harbor there is none. Ships anchor at a distance from the shore, near which there is a reef of rocks with a narrow opening through which rowboats can be pulled in moderate weather. . . . It is no uncommon thing for boats to be dashed by the waves upon the rocks or to be upset, not a few lives being lost.

Pilgrims who made it safely to the shores at Joppa in those days did not have air-conditioned coaches, quality hotels or good highways. Many suffered from improper diet, poor accommodations and the constant demand by the Turks for *fees* to travel over various roads throughout the land.

Prior to the War of Independence, Jaffa was predominantly an Arab community. Fierce battles ensued between the residents of Jaffa and Tel Aviv shortly after the United Nations voted to partition Palestine. But, on the eve of Israel's independence, Jewish forces seized the ancient port city. Leaving behind their homes and possessions, nearly 67,000 Arabs fled Jaffa. It was not long before poor Jewish immigrants permanently claimed the homes of Jaffa's panic-stricken Arabs. However, many Arabs still live in Jaffa today.

Jaffa is a fascinating city to visit. A mosque stands on the traditional site of the house of Simon the tanner at the water's edge. Nearby is the Franciscan Church and Monastery of Saint Peter. An old section of the city has been refurbished and is now occupied by artists' studios and quaint shops. This area and the city's flea market make a most interesting experience for visitors. The port of Jaffa no longer operates.

TEL AVIV

Greater Tel Aviv with its population of over a million people is the largest urban area in Israel. The city and its suburbs continue to grow very rapidly. New industries create demands for housing and related services. Though Tel Aviv and Jaffa are now one city, each still possesses its own unique and distinctive characteristics.

Tel Aviv is the first all-Jewish city in the world. It was founded in 1909 by sixty Jewish families from Jaffa. Its name literally means "Hill of Spring." Though it was founded on twenty-seven acres, the city quickly spread over the nearby sand dunes and hills next to the Mediterranean Sea. However, the primary growth of Tel Aviv was not realized until after World War I when the British seized control of the area from the Turks.

By 1921 Tel Aviv was able to separate from Jaffa and establish its own government. They remained separate cities until 1950. Built entirely in this century, Tel Aviv is very modern. Not unlike other large western cities, many of the streets are wide, the buildings are tall, and the traffic is terrible. Its numerous shops and stores offer the latest in fashion, electronics and western goods. Sidewalk cafes are in abundance, as well as restaurants and bookstores. Tel Aviv's importance as a center of commerce and industry is reflected in its many large office buildings.

Culture is not lacking in Israel, especially in Tel Aviv. The Israeli Philharmonic is based in Tel Aviv's beautiful Mann Auditorium, though concerts are often given in other cities and towns throughout the country. There are several theater groups and an excellent opera company. Visitors and locals enjoy the museums and art galleries. In addition to many lovely parks, Tel Aviv also has a zoo.

The city's beautiful beach area is lined with luxurious hotels whose

Tel Aviv, the first all-Jewish city in the world, with its many beach-front hotels.

standards are among the highest in the world. Most of the hotels are in easy walking distance of Dizengoff Street, Tel Aviv's main shopping area. Tight security around the hotels and beaches is usually maintained by the police and military. One has no fear of walking the streets of Tel Aviv after dark.

Tel Aviv University has grown rapidly since its beginning in 1965. Degrees are offered in the humanities, natural sciences, law, social sciences, medicine, business, education, music and engineering. The University's student body now exceeds 20,000. The Bar-Ilan University is located in Ramat Gan, a suburb of Tel Aviv. It offers a variety of studies, including Judaica, general science, computer science and mathematics.

CAESAREA

Caesarea was founded in 22 B.C. by Herod the Great and named in honor of Caesar Augustus. It took twelve years to complete this port city. The construction of Caesarea's harbor was a masterpiece of engineering. The city was used by Roman procurators for nearly five hundred years. It was a most impressive city with its palaces, temples, theater, hippodrome and baths. Caesarea's main streets were lined with marble statues, and water for the city flowed from the Mount Carmel range through a large aqueduct.

Caesarea has a tumultuous history. The First Jewish Revolt began here in 66 A.D., resulting in the death of nearly all the city's Jews. The city was taken by the Arabs in 640, by the Crusaders in 1101, by Saladin in 1187, again by the Crusaders in 1191, and by the Moslems who destroyed it in 1291.

Peter was summoned from Joppa to visit the home of the Gentile Cornelius who resided in Caesarea (Acts 10). Paul spent over two years in prison at Caesarea before being sent to Rome (Acts 24). It was in this city that Paul made his eloquent appeal to Festus and Agrippa (Acts 25–26).

Caesarea also has a rich church history. In addition to its mention in Acts, the city continued as an important Christian center during the first centuries of the church's life. An important Church Council was held at Caesarea in the second century to regulate the celebration of Easter. Eusebius, church father and historian, was born in

Site of the ancient harbor at Caesarea.

Caesarea in 260. The theologian Origen wrote many of his works here in the third century. In 1101 Crusader King Baldwin I claimed that he found the Holy Grail in Caesarea. It was taken to Italy where it may be seen today in the Cathedral of Saint Lorenzo in Genoa. Excavations begun in 1956 at Caesarea unearthed some outstanding finds. Most of the visible ruins are from the Crusader period, but many of the ancient Roman ruins were used by the Crusaders in the foundations of their less durable and less impressive structures. Portions of the Crusader wall with its deep moat and fortifications stand today in rather excellent condition. Ruins in the harbor itself are also visible, and are currently undergoing excavation.

The Roman theater at Caesarea was uncovered in 1961. It is, by far, the most impressive structure unearthed in the city. Restored, it is used today for various programs and concerts. Some of the original seats in the theater still remain.

Other important archaeological finds include statuary and a stone inscribed with the name of Pontius Pilate. A short distance from the primary ruins of Caesarea are the remnants of an ancient Roman aqueduct and a Roman hippodrome which had a seating capacity of 20,000.

The modern town of Caesarea typifies modern suburbia with its lovely single-family homes and Israel's only golf course.

HAIFA

Haifa, the third-largest city in Israel, is not mentioned in Scripture because it was not established until the second century A.D. The city was first mentioned in Talmudic literature during the third century. It was of some importance until destroyed by the Crusaders; afterwards, its neighbor Acre overshadowed it completely. When the Turks began their rule over Palestine in 1517, Haifa was only a small village and remained so throughout much of their occupation. However, by the beginning of the twentieth century, Zionist Jews had significantly developed the port city. When Haifa was captured by Israel on April 22, 1948, most of its 76,000 Arab residents fled into Lebanon.

Located on the Mediterranean coast, Haifa is a busy and prosperous port. Its bay and docks are usually filled with commercial and

A panoramic view of Haifa.

military vessels, as well as cruise ships. The Israeli Navy has a base here, and the U.S. Sixth Fleet uses Haifa as an official port-of-call. The port handles nearly half of the nation's cargo. The city is also known for its heavy industry, oil refineries and grain elevators. Its largest grain elevator, Dagon, is 230 feet high and holds 100,000 tons of grain. A large power station is also located in Haifa, along with numerous factories producing glass, fertilizers, chemicals, textiles and furniture.

The population of Haifa now exceeds 250,000, with another 200,000 in the surrounding area. Not many years ago, most of Haifa's residents lived on the narrow coastal strip between the Mediterranean and the Mount Carmel range, but today much of the city is located on Mount Carmel itself. Impressive new apartment buildings, homes and businesses are built along the winding streets of Mount Carmel's western side which offers the residents a magnificent view. A subway completed in 1959 runs from the harbor to the top of Mount Carmel.

Haifa is home to Israel's Institute of Technology, known more commonly as Technion. Situated on a 300-acre campus on Mount Carmel, the Technion is the oldest institution of higher learning in the country. More than 17,000 students are enrolled in its undergraduate programs. The Technion provides over two-thirds of Israel's engineers. Another center of learning is the University of Haifa, founded in 1963. It has an enrollment of over 5,000 undergraduate students.

A landmark of the city is the Bahai Shrine on the lower slopes of Mount Carmel. Its golden-domed sanctuary and beautiful gardens attract many visitors. The Bahai religion was founded in the mid-nineteenth century by Mirza Ali-Muhammad. Bahai means "glory" in Arabic. They believe that "all great world religions are valid revelations of truth from the Infinite Source."

MOUNT CARMEL

The Carmel range runs along the northern part of Israel's coast for fifteen miles. The height of the Carmel range varies from 470 feet at the coast to 1791 feet at its highest point. The Carmel mountain range which remains green throughout the year was well-known in the Scriptures for its vineyards. Its name comes from the Hebrew *Karem-El*, meaning "Vineyard of God."

Carmel is mentioned in Joshua as the boundary for the territory of Asher (Joshua 19:24). It is best remembered in Scripture as the scene of Elijah's contest with the prophets of Baal (1 Kings 18). Other biblical references to Mount Carmel include Song of Solomon 7:5, Amos 1:2 and 9:3, Jeremiah 46:18 and 50:19, and Isaiah 35:2.

Two Carmelite monasteries whose patron saint is Elijah are situated on Mount Carmel. Stella Maris Monastery stands on the northwest summit overlooking the bay of Haifa. A church on the monastery grounds, dedicated to the Virgin Mary, is built over a cave where some believe Elijah hid when he fled from King Ahab during the famine. The Stella Maris Monastery served as a hospital for Napoleon's wounded troops during his unsuccessful attempt to capture Acre from the Turks in 1799. Several of Napoleon's soldiers are buried at the monastery's front entrance. The second Carmelite monastery, known as the Monastery of Saint Elijah (Muhraka, Place of Burning), is located on top of the southeastern slope of Mount Carmel on the traditional site where Elijah called down fire in his contest with the prophets of Baal.

ACRE

Perhaps second only to Jerusalem in historical importance is the port city of Acre (Acco, Akko). First appearing in Egyptian literature in the fourteenth century B.C., a strategic location and excellent port made it a prize to be claimed by various rulers and nations throughout the centuries. When it was occupied by the Greeks and Romans, the city was known as Ptolemais. It is mentioned by that name in Acts 21: 7 in reference to a brief visit by Paul.

Acre became an important Arab stronghold and port following its conquest in 638 A.D. The Crusaders captured the city in 1104 and renamed it Saint Jean d' Acre. Because of its strategic importance against any attempted invasion by sea, the Crusaders strengthened the fortifications and walls. Saladin forced the Crusaders out of Acre in 1187, but he could not hold out against the forces of Richard the Lion-Heart of England and Philippe Auguste of France when they came to Acre leading the forces of the second Crusade in 1191. Acre

Acre, the ancient port city of the Crusaders.

remained under the control of the Crusaders until 1291 when they were permanently driven from Palestine by the Mamelukes. Fearing that other foreigners might try to invade Palestine by securing Acre, the Mamelukes destroyed the city.

Ahmed Pasha Jazzar, known as "the Butcher," was ruling Acre when Napoleon attempted his invasion of Palestine in 1799. Jazzar strengthened the walls of Acre and increased its fortifications. Much of what is seen today is from his time, although Crusader ruins also remain. One of the most outstanding mosques in Israel today is the Mosque of Ahmed al-Jazzar located in Acre.

The British captured the city in 1918, but its importance diminished with the development of Haifa. Under the British Mandate, Acre became infamous for its prison in the eighteenth-century Citadel. Hundreds of Jews were incarcerated there, including Moshe Dayan, and eight Jews were hanged on the gallows in the Citadel.

Israel captured Acre from the Arabs on May 17, 1948. Today the population of the city, including Arabs, exceeds 40,000.

NAHARIYA

A short distance north of Acre is the picturesque town of Nahariya, founded in 1934 by German Jews who fled the terrors of Hitler. The tree-lined streets, horse-drawn carriages, sidewalk cafes and quaint shops give Nahariya the atmosphere and appearance of a small European town.

A Canaanite temple dedicated to the Phoenician goddess Asherah was discovered in Nahariya. Excavations were conducted from 1947 to 1955.

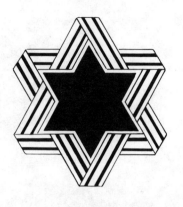

ישראל

ISRAEL

The People Of Israel

Jewish children ready for another day of school.

The People Of Israel

Jews comprise nearly 84 percent of Israel's population. The other 16 percent are mostly Arabs, though many other nationalities and races live in the Jewish state as well. It is estimated that 1,400,000 Arabs now reside in the occupied territories. The peoples and cultures represented in Israel are amazingly diverse. This surprises many visitors who tend to group all Arabs and Jews into two specific molds. The truth is that Jews in Israel differ from each other in culture and lifestyle as much as they differ from the Arabs. Likewise, even some Arabs in Israel and in the occupied territories have very different cultures from one another. Jews are held together in a cohesive unit largely through their common loyalty to the State of Israel, while the Arabs are bonded chiefly as Palestinians. Because the cultures, mores and backgrounds of Israel's people are so diverse and complicated, it is possible only to give some general impressions.

JEWS

There has been a Jewish presence in Israel since the days of the Patriarchs. Even when the Jews were scattered during their exiles (diaspora), some always remained in the land. Most Jews in Israel today came in several waves of immigration (aliya). The momentum of immigration began at the end of the last century, then accelerated during the first half of the present century. But it was not until the State of Israel was established in 1948 that the greatest wave of immigration occurred. Between 1948 and 1951, more than 754,000 Jews immigrated to Israel from various nations of the world. Thousands of Soviet Jews have settled in Israel since 1960.

Jews born in Israel are called "sabras." Sabra is a cactus plant in

Israel which bears a fruit that is "prickly on the outside but sweet on the inside." This definition has been commonly applied to Israel's native-born sons and daughters.

Because Jews in Israel today come from so many countries of the world, numerous languages are spoken. However, all immigrants are offered lessons in Hebrew, the official language of the nation. Though the cultures and lifestyles are very diverse, Israel's Jews may be viewed in three basic groups: Ashkenazim, Sephardim and Oriental.

The Ashkenazim are mainly Jews with European, American, and South African backgrounds. Many of the Ashkenazim speak Yiddish, a combination of Hebrew and German. The ultra-orthodox, called Hassidim, wear long black coats and fur-trimmed hats.

The Sephardim came chiefly from Spain, Portugal and and North Africa. Their native language is Ladino, a combination of Hebrew and Spanish, but only the older Sephardim speak this language today. Until the present century, most of the Jews in Palestine were Sephardim.

The Oriental Jews are mostly from countries of the Middle East. Shortly after the State of Israel was established in 1948, more than 45,000 Jews were airlifted to Israel from Yemen in "Operation Magic Carpet." These Yemenite Jews have their own rituals and customs, many of which have been influenced by Arab culture.

Most Jews in Israel are not religious. They seldom go to synagogue, read the Scriptures or practice Judaism in any way, viewing themselves first and foremost as Israelis. Religious Jews have many different theological views and practices from ultra-liberal to ultra-orthodox. The Jews who are most orthodox wear sidelocks and clothes which are styled in the last century. Many ultra-orthodox wives shave their heads and then cover them with a kerchief so that they do not appear attractive to other men. Some ultra-orthodox Jews live in the Mea Shearim section of West Jerusalem, near the Old City and the Western Wall. One group among the ultra-orthodox, the Neturei Karta, refuses to recognize the State of Israel, convinced that the Messiah himself will come and establish the nation. They are deeply offended by all human efforts to establish the Jewish state. Sometimes they are militant regarding this position and their opposition to Zionism.

While religious Jews represent only a minority of Israel's population, they have still been able to greatly influence nearly every aspect of the nation's life and structure through their representatives in the Knesset. There are more than 6,000 synagogues in Israel and over 400 state-supported rabbis. Jewish dietary laws are observed in the Israeli armed forces, as well as in most Jewish hotels and restaurants. There is little or no public transportation on the Sabbath (Shabbat), and even El Al, the Israeli airline, serves only kosher meals and is forbidden to operate on the Sabbath. Cars which dare to venture into the ultra-orthodox neighborhoods on the Sabbath are frequently stoned. There is constant tension between the secular and religious Jews of Israel over these and other issues, but so far the religious minority controls the secular majority on many matters.

Shabbat (Sabbath) is observed from Friday night to Saturday sundown. Six days Israeli businesses and industries function, but on the Sabbath all are closed. It is a day of rest and relaxation with family and friends, as well as a day of prayer. Jewish holy days which are observed in Israel include: Rosh Hashana (New Year), Yom Kippur (Day of Atonement), Hanukkah (Festival of Lights), Purim (Deliverence), Pesach (Passover), Shavuot (Pentecost, Feast of Weeks), and Succot (Feast of Tabernacles).

THE SAMARITANS

At the turn of the twentieth century, the Samaritans numbered less than 150, but in recent years their population has increased to nearly 500. They reside at Holon, near Tel Aviv, and in Nablus (ancient Shechem).

Socially and religiously, the Samaritans go back to the 8th century B.C. when Assyria sent settlers into northern Israel after its fall. These settlers intermarried with the people of Israel, mixing traditions and religions.

Their religious life is extremely strict. Marriage to persons outside their own community, except to Jews who agree to accept the Samaritan faith, is forbidden. They accept only the first five books of the Bible and hold Mount Gerizim as their center of worship. According to their teachings, they are descended from the tribes of Ephraim and Manasseh.

THE ARABS

The majority of Arabs living in Israel, the West Bank and the Gaza Strip are Sunni Moslems. There are more than 200 Moslem clergy within Israel proper paid by the State and over 100 mosques, the most important being the Al Aksa Mosque located on the Temple Mount. The Arabs operate their own schools which use the Arabic language within Israel and the occupied territories. They also publish their own newspaper. Israeli Arabs have representation in the Knesset. Several thousand Arabs are enrolled in Israel's universities.

In the West Bank and Gaza Strip, Arabs once elected their own town and village leaders, but now those leaders are appointed by the Israeli authorities who govern the territories. They had their own police units until the uprisings in 1987-1988, but during these struggles many of the Arab police resigned in protest. For the most part, the Arabs living within Israel proper tend to identify with the Arabs on the West Bank and in the Gaza Strip. The economic status of Arabs living in Israel and in the occupied territories is vastly superior to the condition of Arabs in neighboring countries.

Family life is strong and male dominated within the Arab society. Women are gradually achieving more status, but they basically still function in subservient roles. Because of their religion and culture, the Arabs have a high birthrate.

The Moslem religion was founded in the seventh century A.D. by Mohammed. Even so, the Moslems trace their lineage to Abraham. Their great profession of faith, the Shahada, declares: "There is no God but God (Allah), and Mohammed is his prophet."

Basic to the Moslem faith is the belief that God has given four primary revelations to man- the Torah, the Psalms of David, the Gospels of Jesus, and the Koran. For Moslems, the Koran is the most important and complete of the four revelations. To Moslems, Jesus is a prophet, nothing more.

Like Jews, Moslem males are circumcised. Unlike the Jews, the Moslem sabbath is on Friday, a change made specifically by Mohammed. Each Friday the Moslems prepare themselves for worship by ceremonial cleansing. Their worship consists mostly of prayers, readings from the Koran and preaching. Since they are required to pray in the direction of Mecca, their most holy city, a niche is carved

Arab boy in the Old City.

out in the wall of each mosque or shrine to confirm the proper direction.

Five times each day the Moslems are called to prayer from a minaret. The deeply religious answer these calls, stopping whatever they may be doing in order to pray. In years past most calls to prayer were made through the human voice, but in these days of modern technology the calls are more likely to be pre-recorded, activated by timers and played over loud-speakers.

Five Pillars of Islam outline a rather simplistic expression of religious duty:

1. Witness to the oneness of God and Mohammed as his prophet.
2. Pray five times each day in the proper manner.
3. Fast during the month of Ramadan.
4. Give alms.
5. Make a pilgrimage (haj) to Mecca at least once in a lifetime.

THE BEDOUIN

Of the more than 75,000 Bedouin living in Israel today, 45,000 are located in the Negev. The others are scattered over the country as far north as Galilee. In Arabic, *Bedouin* means "sons of the desert." While most Bedouin wander over the land raising sheep, goats and camels, some have more recently begun to build permanent homes.

The Bedouin are divided into tribes headed by a sheikh. In routine internal matters, they are permitted to carry out their own justice. Bedouin justice can be very severe, especially where family honor is at stake.

Children are given little discipline up to the age of seven; however, from that age they are carefully taught Bedouin ways. Boys and girls at age thirteen begin to assume adult responsibilities. Between the ages of sixteen and twenty they are permitted to marry. Marriages, often between first cousins, are prearranged by the parents. The Bedouin are very prolific, reflecting their cultural and religious beliefs. Some men even have several wives, so those family units can be quite large. However, Bedouin families in Israel have recently become smaller due mostly to poor nutrition and lack of protein. Bedouin women are subservient to their husbands, but they are honored and protected. Daughters are especially watched over by their fathers and brothers, and sexual misconduct by unmarried girls is a grievous offense.

Bedouin are known to be very courteous and hospitable. They are generous hosts who would never turn a stranger away from their tents.

THE DRUZE

Two villages on Mount Carmel belong to a religious sect known as the Druze. Their religion dates to the eleventh century when they broke away from Islam. Since the Druze religious beliefs are kept secret, little is known about them, except that they combine Moslem, Jewish and Christian thought, and that Jethro, father-in-law of Moses, is their patron prophet. Women have a place of honor in their society, and may be chosen as religious leaders.

There are presently 45,000 Druze living in Israel. They live in eighteen villages located on Mount Carmel, in Galilee and on the Golan Heights. Though Arab-speaking, they have maintained an excellent relationship with the Israelis. The Druze have been made full citizens of Israel. By their own choice, their young people serve in the Israeli military. They operate their own schools and courts.

CHRISTIANS

The nearly 90,000 Christians living in Israel today account for only 2.9 percent of the total population. Most of the Christians are Arabs living in Nazareth and Jerusalem. The majority of Christians in Israel are either Melkites (Greek Catholics), Roman Catholic or Greek Orthodox. While there are only 300 churches and chapels in Israel, there are over 2200 clergy, including 400 monks and 850 nuns.

Protestants in Israel number less than 4,000. Several major denominations have some type of presence in Israel or the West Bank. Lutherans have significant works in Jerusalem and the West Bank. The Baptists maintain ministries in Jerusalem, Nazareth and elsewhere throughout the country. There are any number of independent evangelical ministries operating throughout the general region as well, including the Christian Embassy in Jerusalem.

Several religious sects are established in Israel. The Mormon sect recently constructed a center on the Mount of Olives, but not before giving assurances to Israeli authorities that they would not attempt to win converts. All Christian ministries and religious sects which are focused at the conversion of Jews and Arabs face strong opposition in Israel. In 1977 the Knesset passed a law making it a crime to convert people to other religions through use of bribes. Just what constitutes a *bribe* is unclear.

There are small groups of Messianic Jews in Israel who have accepted Jesus Christ as their Lord and Savior. While these groups have experienced some growth, there are not significant numbers of Jews who are responding to the Christian message. This does not seem to discourage those who sense a clear mandate from the Scripture to witness the Gospel to the Jews.

THE KIBBUTZ

In the early part of this century, settlers in Palestine faced tremendous obstacles in their development of the land. Draining malaria-infested swamps, building irrigation systems and providing adequate defense against terrorists were all tasks too large for individuals or families. The solution for these and other problems came through the establishment of collective settlements known as the kibbutzim (kibbutz, singular). The philosophy of the kibbutzim is simple- *Each member works according to his ability and receives according to his needs*.

Kibbutzim are operated on land leased from the government. Some kibbutzim have as few as a dozen persons in their community, while three or four have as many as two or three thousand. The primary purposes of a kibbutz are to develop the land, strengthen the State of Israel, and provide a good life for its members based on equality and social justice.

Each kibbutz is governed democratically by a general assembly of all members. Committees and administrators are elected to direct the business affairs of the settlement. The committees make decisions regarding work assignments, finances, education, recreation, and care of the facilities. Kibbutz members seldom need personal money because everything is provided. Each year individuals and families of the kibbutz are given paid vacations, and some even offer vacations abroad.

Life on a kibbutz in years past required much hard work and considerable personal sacrifice. The hard work is still plentiful on the kibbutzim, but the living conditions have greatly improved. The quarters vary in size, but each family is given an adequate home. Most of the housing units are extremely lovely with plenty of green lawns and flowers. The average kibbutz has community buildings and schools, and some have swimming pools, gyms, and auditoriums where plays and concerts are presented.

Children are still housed separately from their parents in many kibbutzim, but family life is extremely important. Each day the parents and children spend quality time together. While the parents work, the children are in school or some type of child-care program, but from late afternoon until bedtime, parents and children are together. Young people on the kibbutz who desire to go to college or the university submit their request to the appropriate committee. If approved, they will have all their expenses paid by the kibbutz.

The primary focus of each kibbutz was farming until recent years; however, many now operate various types of industry as their primary source of income. A number of the kibbutzim cater to tourists by providing quality motels and restaurants. Some manufacture furniture, housewares, and other essentials. Still others operate heavy industry or manufacture electronic equipment.

Israel's kibbutzim and farms now produce 85 percent of the nation's food requirements. Some of the Israeli kibbutzim have the highest yields per acre in the world. Agricultural crops include a wide variety of citrus, wheat, corn, cotton and tobacco. Beef and dairy cattle, sheep and goats, chickens and turkeys are all raised in abundance in Israel. As in Bible times, olive groves are found throughout the country. Vineyards grow on the slopes of Mount Carmel and elsewhere, producing quality wines which are exported throughout the world.

Membership requirements in the kibbutzim can be rather strict. After serving a one-year period of probation, individuals are accepted or rejected through a vote of the entire community. Members may leave anytime, but they may take only their personal belongings since all property, including clothing, belongs to the kibbutz. Those who leave receive a cash settlement based on the number of years they were members. Aged members are permitted to retire when deemed appropriate and are cared for on the kibbutz for as long as they live.

Today there are 275 kibbutzim in Israel, representing about two percent of the total population. Kibbutz members have had an outstanding record of service in the government and the military. A large number of pilots in the Israeli Air Force, as well as many members of the Knesset, were born and raised in the kibbutzim.

THE MOSHAV

Another agricultural community in Israel is the moshav (moshavim, plural). Unlike the kibbutzim, members of the moshav own their individual homes and farms. They join together to cultivate community lands, sell produce and purchase equipment. Each moshav has a general assembly which elects a council to administer its affairs, receive new members, and approve all transfers of farms. There are 412 moshavim in Israel today.

MOSHAV SHITUFI

A moshav shitufi is a collective where land and economy are controlled by the community in a manner similar to the kibbutzim. However, each family has full responsibility for its own household and children. Work assignments and income are based on individual needs and circumstances. Israel has 47 moshav shitufi. Degania, the first collective settlement in Israel and a moshav shitufi, was founded in 1909 on the shores of Lake Gennesaret. Nes Amin, a moshav shitufi, is a Christian settlement.

THE ISRAEL DEFENSE FORCES

Israel's efficient and well-trained armed forces are known and respected throughout the world. In the Six Day War of 1967, the world watched in amazement as Israel's forces moved with skill and determination to defeat five heavily armed Arab nations. And who can forget the genius of Israel's raid on Entebbe, July 4, 1976, when the IDF rescued over a hundred hostages? Israel's forces are the best equipped and the best trained in the Middle East. They have to be. If defeated, the Arab armies can live to fight another day. With one lost war, Israel is finished as a nation.

While the United States and other European nations have supplied Israel with highly technical and sophisticated armaments, the Israelis have developed the capability to build highly competitive fighter planes, tanks, ships and guns. And in the last few years it has been presumed that Israel has developed a nuclear capability.

In 1948 Israel's Provisional Government formed the Israel Defense Forces (IDF) by bringing together several independent Jewish defense organizations. Although the IDF is under one administration, it has three basic units- army, navy and air force. There are also three regional commands- northern, central and southern. Each is headed by a regional commander who holds the rank of Major-General. The entire IDF is led by the Chief of Staff who is under the authority of the Minister of Defense and the Cabinet.

Men between the ages of 18 and 39 are drafted for thirty-six months of active duty. Unmarried women between the ages of 18 and 29 are drafted for twenty-four months of active duty. Men serve in the reserves until age 55; women serve in the reserves until age 34, but only a few specialists are actually called to active duty. The men are required to report for thirty-one days of annual training until age 40, although many are called for much longer periods. A few Arabs, Christians and Moslems serve voluntarily in the IDF. The Druze voluntarily committed themselves to the same draft requirements as Jews.

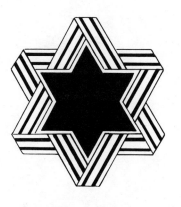

ישראל

ISRAEL

Israel, Land Of Prophecy

Israel, Land Of Prophecy

INTRODUCTION

It is appropriate at the outset of any discussion on prophecy for the reader to understand the author's attitude toward Scripture as well as his views regarding prophecy. From my youth, I have believed and acknowledged the Bible to be the infallible and inerrant Word of God, fully trustworthy in all that it teaches. It is my further belief that the best commentary on the Bible is Scripture itself. Therefore, I shall endeavor to allow Scripture to speak for itself regarding the prophetical events considered. With regard to my views on prophecy, I hold with deep conviction to a premillennial view of Christ's return. Further, I believe that Israel is the earthly centerpiece of all prophetic movement in reference to our Lord's soon coming in glory.

Because the Bible is God's revelation to man, we may be confident in its message concerning future events. The apostle Peter tells us:

> Above all, you must understand that no prophecy of Scripture came about by the prophet's own interpretation. For prophecy never had its origin in the will of man, but men spoke from God as they were carried along by the Holy Spirit
> *(2 Peter 1:20–21).*

According to Scripture, the key test for all prophetic revelation is its fulfillment.

> You may say to yourselves, "How can we know when a message has not been spoken by the Lord?" If what a prophet proclaims in the name of the Lord does not take place or come

true, that is a message the Lord has not spoken. That prophet has spoken presumptuously. Do not be afraid of him
(Deuteronomy 18:21–22).

There are literally thousands of fulfilled prophecies in both the Old and New Testaments regarding the first and second comings of Christ, as well as events involving the restoration of the nation and land of Israel.

Scripture should be taken literally or at face value wherever possible. Where it is obvious that symbols, similes, and metaphors have been used for instructional purposes, the thoughtful Bible student will treat the text accordingly. However, most, if not all, fulfilled prophecies of Scripture related to Jesus' first coming had an obvious literalness about them. Why should we assume it would be otherwise regarding His second coming or in relationship to Israel? For example, Isaiah foretold that Jesus would be born of a virgin (7:14). Micah foretold that the Messiah would be born in Bethlehem and come from the tribe of Judah (5:2). Hosea detailed the flight of the holy family into Egypt (11:1). Jeremiah gave the harsh but accurate prophecy of Bethlehem's children being destroyed (31:15). Hundreds of years before the event, Zechariah detailed Jesus' entry into Jerusalem on that first Palm Sunday (9:9). And long before crucifixions were known, David prophetically reported in detail the manner of Jesus' death on the cross (Psalm 22). These are only a few illustrations of the literal statement and the literal fulfillment of biblical prophecies.

Following His resurrection, Jesus met two disciples on the road to Emmaus. Instead of simply presenting *Himself* to them as the primary evidence of His resurrection, He chose to bring them to faith through *the reality of Scriptures*. Though He stood before them in His resurrected body, He required their faith to be awakened in the same manner as ours must be awakened, namely, through the Word of God.

He said to them , "How foolish you are, and how slow of heart to believe all that the prophets have spoken! Did not the Messiah have to suffer these things and then enter his glory?" And beginning with Moses and all the Prophets, he explained to them what was said in all the Scriptures concerning himself
(Luke 24:25–27).

After Jesus had left them, the two disciples responded:

> Were not our hearts burning within us while he talked with us
> on the road and opened the Scriptures to us?
>
> *(Luke 24:32).*

Luke records the same truth in his account of a later appearance to
Christ's eleven disciples.

> He said to them, "This is what I told you while I was still with
> you: Everything must be fulfilled that is written about me in the
> Law of Moses, the Prophets and the Psalms." Then he opened
> their minds so they could understand the Scriptures
>
> *(Luke 24:44-45).*

These prophecies were not fulfilled by Jesus simply through some
mechanical attention to detail; they were fulfilled because He "hum-
bled himself and became obedient to death- even death on a cross!"
(Philippians 2:8).

Most liberal theologians believe that the book of Daniel was written around 165 B.C. and that Daniel was only a character from Israel's folklore. Yet, in His Mount Olivet discourse (Matthew 24), Jesus identifies Daniel as a prophet. And where is the liberal
theologian today who will even dare to suggest that Noah might have
been an historical person? But in the Mount Olivet discourse Jesus
acknowledged the historicity of Noah. Furthermore, in that same
prophetic utterance, He told of the blossoming fig tree (Israel). The
basic issue facing students of Scripture is not the interpretation of the
text, though often difficult, but whether or not we believe the text.

Finally, there are those who would tell us that God's dealings with
the nation of Israel ended at the time of their rejection of Yeshua (Jesus) as the Messiah. There is not a shred of evidence in the Bible to
support such a claim. On the contrary, the Bible teaches that God
made an *eternal covenant* with Abraham and his descendants
through Isaac and Jacob. Both the Old and New Testaments are re-
plete with references concerning God's scattering the nation of Israel
and regathering them in the last days.

My conclusions are these:

1. The Bible is fully God's Word and true in all it teaches.
2. Thousands of biblical prophecies regarding Jesus' first coming were literally given and literally fulfilled. The same holds true regarding prophecies about Israel. Therefore, where possible, we should assume a literal fulfillment of prophecies relating to Jesus' second coming and relating to Israel.
3. The writers of the New Testament, under the inspiration of the Holy Spirit, interpreted for us the fulfillment of many obscure passages of prophecy, such as Isaiah 7:14, and they pointed out numerous explicit prophecies definitely fulfilled. Fulfillment of some prophecies assures the final fulfillment of all.
4. Jesus Himself acknowledged the literal fulfillment of Old Testament prophecies pertaining to Himself and Israel. As He acknowledged the authenticity of various persons in the Bible, we may have confidence in all that He tells us in Scripture.
5. Israel is precious to the Lord. His covenant with Abraham, Isaac and Jacob is *eternal* and will be honored. As Israel was scattered through divine judgment because of their disobedience, today they are being regathered in fulfillment of Holy Scripture. The Church and Israel have a spiritual unity in the person of the Lord Jesus Christ, but God's plan for each is separate.

GOD'S COVENANT WITH ABRAHAM

Twentieth-century Israel is an enigma to many. Aside from God's covenant with the Patriarchs, there is no rational explanation for Israel's survival through centuries of exile and persecution. By every conceivable measure, Israel should have been finished as a nation, if not during the Babylonian exile, certainly during the nearly two millenniums which followed the destruction of the Temple and Jerusalem in 70 A.D. Yet after almost two thousand years of exile, they are in their land with language, religion, culture and hopes undimmed.

There is an unmistakable connection between Israel of the twentieth century and Abraham, Isaac, Jacob and David. The covenant of God with the Patriarchs and David is for His Name's sake. It was part of His plan to bring redemption to mankind through Israel. God's covenant with the Patriarchs and David was unconditional. It was never based on their agreement, but only upon God's promises to them. God's conditional covenant with Israel came through Moses and centered on their continuance in the land itself. Yet when Israel's disobedience caused her dispersion among the nations of the world in 586 B.C. and in 70 A.D., the same disobedience never nullified God's unbreakable promises to Abraham, Isaac, Jacob and David.

GOD'S COVENANT REGARDING THE LAND

Before Abraham left Ur of the Chaldees, God told him:

Leave your country, your people and your father's household and go to the land I will show you. I will make your name great, and you will be a blessing. I will bless those who bless you, and whoever curses you I will curse; and all peoples on earth will be blessed through you

(Genesis 12:1-3).

After Abraham's arrival in the land, God again spoke to him: "To your offspring I will give this land" (Genesis 12:7). A short time later God told Abraham, "Go, walk through the length and breadth of the land, for I am giving it to you" (Genesis 13:17). At the time God promised to give Abraham an heir, He further informed Abraham that his descendants would go into exile for four hundred years, and only then would they take possession of the Promised Land. Israel's exile into Egypt came as no surprise to God, nor was He surprised at their exodus from Egypt under the leadership of Moses.

Abraham was given the specific boundaries of Israel.

On that day the Lord made a covenant with Abram and said, "To your descendants I give this land, from the river of Egypt to the great river, the Euphrates- the land of the Kenites, Kenizzites, Kadmonites, Hittites, Perizzites, Rephaites, Amorites, Canaanites, Girgashites and Jebusites"

(Genesis 15:18-21).

195

Surely this is a promise which is yet to be fulfilled in literal, permanent fashion. The only time Israel even came close to controlling all of the promised territory was under the reign of Solomon. But there is no reason to assume that these boundaries should be viewed other than literally.

THE COVENANT GIVEN THROUGH
ISAAC AND JACOB

At age ninety-nine, Abraham was visited by the Lord who reaffirmed the covenant to him.

> The whole of the land of Canaan, where you are now an alien,
> I will give as an everlasting possession to you and your descendants after you; and I will be their God
>
> *(Genesis 17:8).*

God specified that Abraham's inheritance would extend only through his son Isaac, and from Isaac through Jacob. The covenant with Abraham was repeated to Isaac (Genesis 26:4) and again to Jacob (Genesis 28: 13-15).

COVENANT HONORED EVEN IN DISOBEDIENCE

God reaffirmed His sure covenant with Abraham even in times of judgment and exile. At the time of the Babylonian exile and in the midst of Israel's rebellion, God spoke through the prophet Jeremiah:

> This is what the Lord says,
> he who appoints the sun to shine by day,
> who decrees the moon and stars to shine by night,
> who stirs up the sea so that its waves roar-
> the Lord Almighty is his name:
> Only if these decrees vanish from my sight,
> declares the Lord, will the descendants of Israel
> ever cease to be a nation before me *(31:35-36).*

God's unbreakable promise to Abraham is the theme of Hebrews 6:13-18. In Romans 9, 10 and 11, Paul assures the Church that God still has a plan and a place for Israel.

GOD'S COVENANT WITH DAVID

As Abraham was promised an everlasting covenant through his descendants, so David was also promised that his throne and kingdom would endure forever. In Psalm 89 God declared:

I have sworn to David my servant, I will establish your line forever and make your throne firm through all generations (3–4).

According to Isaiah, this covenant is fulfilled through Jesus Christ who will one day reign unendingly on the throne of David.

For to us a child is born, to us a son is given,
and the government will be on his shoulders.
And he will be called Wonderful Counselor,
Mighty God, Everlasting Father, Prince of Peace.
Of the increase of his government and peace
there will be no end. He will reign on David's
throne and over his kingdom . . . forever (9:6–7).

In a passage directly related to Israel's return from exile, God declared through Jeremiah:

"The days are coming," declares the Lord, "when I will raise up to David a righteous Branch, a King who will reign wisely and do what is just and right in the land. In his days Judah will be saved and Israel will live in safety. This is the name by which he will be called: The Lord our Righteousness" (23:5–6).

It is clear from these and many other passages that God's intention was always to honor His covenant with the Patriarchs and David.

THE DISPERSION OF THE JEWS

The Jews refer to their exile from the land of Israel as the *diaspora*. The first exile came in 722 B.C. when the northern tribes were carried off by Assyria. The southern kingdom was exiled to Babylon for seventy years starting in 604 B.C. The final conquest and destruction of Jerusalem in 586 B.C. by Nebuchadnezzar is described in 2 Chronicles 36. The reason for their exile is best summarized in verses 15 and 16:

> The Lord, the God of their fathers, sent word to them through his messengers again and again, because he had pity on his people and on his dwelling place. But they mocked God's messengers, despised his words and scoffed at his prophets until the wrath of the Lord was aroused against his people and there was no remedy.

The Assyrian Captivity was foretold by Isaiah (chapter 7). In 2 Kings 17 the reasons for the captivity are clearly stated:

> All this took place because the Israelites had sinned against the Lord their God. . . . They worshiped other gods and followed the practices of the nations the Lord had driven out before them, as well as the practices that the kings of Israel had introduced (7–8).

Because the northern tribes never returned from exile, they are often referred to as the "lost tribes of Israel."

The Babylonian Captivity was prophesied by many prophets, but especially Jeremiah who was known as "the weeping prophet." Jeremiah also prophesied the return of the Jews from Babylon:

> This is what the Lord says: "When seventy years are completed for Babylon, I will come to you and fulfill my gracious promise to bring you back to this place. For I know the plans I have for you," declares the Lord, "plans to prosper you and not to harm you, plans to give you hope and a future"
>
> *(Jeremiah 29:10–11).*

THE DIASPORA IN 70 A.D.

At the time of Jesus, the Jews truly believed that God would never permit the Temple to be destroyed again (Jeremiah 7). But, in His prophecy concerning Jerusalem, Jesus made it clear that because of Israel's rebellion "not one stone would be left on another" (Matthew 24:1-2). Speaking of Jerusalem, Luke wrote:

As he approached Jerusalem and saw the city, he wept over it and said, "If you, even you, had only known on this day what would bring you peace- but now it is hidden from your eyes. The days will come upon you when your enemies will build an embankment against you and encircle you and hem you in on every side. They will dash you to the ground, you and the children within your walls. They will not leave one stone on another, because you did not recognize the time of God's coming to you

(Luke 19:41-44).

According to Jesus, the fundamental reason for Israel's destruction and exile was her rejection of the promised Messiah.

Jesus' prophecies regarding Jerusalem were given with amazing detail nearly forty years prior to their fulfillment. It is no wonder that He wept over the city. When the Roman legions besieged Jerusalem in 70 A.D. under the command of Titus, they first assembled on the very mountain where Jesus foretold Jerusalem's destruction. The Jews were walled in from the reach of Titus during the siege, but he encircled the city so that none could escape, just as Jesus had said. In order to gain entrance to Jerusalem, the Romans built an "embankment" against the city's northern wall, exactly as foretold by Jesus. Over one million Jews died in the siege of Jerusalem. The starvation and pain among the inhabitants within the city's walls, as described by Josephus Flavius, were so severe that they resorted to cannibalism. A prophecy in Deuteronomy described the scene in detail.

Because of the suffering that your enemy will inflict on you during the siege, you will eat the fruit of the womb, the flesh of the sons and daughters the Lord your God has given you. Even the most gentle and sensitive man among you will have no compassion on his own brother or the wife he loves or his surviving children, and he will not give to one of them any of the flesh of his children that he is eating (28:53-55).

The second revolt a few decades later was nearly as costly in lives as the first revolt had been, especially in relation to Jerusalem. Over 500,000 Jews were killed between 132 and 135 A.D. Many died dur-

199

ing the siege and destruction of Jerusalem. After this revolt, most of the remaining Jews were banished from the country.

LIFE DURING THE DIASPORA

The Jews scattered to nations throughout the world following the destruction of Jerusalem in 70 A.D., and again in 135 A.D., though some did remain in Israel, mostly in the northern part initially. There were those who found their host countries to be extremely hospitable; however, most found life very difficult. Sometimes the Jews were accepted for a season, but inevitably the persecutions would begin.

Life for the Jews during the Crusades was anything but secure. In both Europe and Palestine, thousands of Jews were killed by Crusaders who thought they were doing God a favor. "Deus Vult," they cried ("God wills it").

In 1215 the Fourth Lateran Council required all Jews to wear badges as identification. Their lands and personal property were confiscated. Spain became a haven for Jews in the Middle Ages when persecution in Europe forced them to flee. For nearly two centuries, the Jews of Spain mingled freely, adding much to Spanish life, both in academics and culture. But decades of peace ended with the Spanish Inquisition when thousands of Jews were forced to choose between Christianity, exile or death. During the reign of Ferdinand and Isabella, nearly a million Jews were exiled, which meant for many to be placed on boats and set adrift to die at sea. As Columbus set sail for America in 1492, he passed several of these Jewish death boats in the harbor.

In Russia and Poland the Jews lived in peace for decades, but then came the *pogroms* when they were systematically persecuted. Many fled from Russia to the United States and Great Britain. Some went to Palestine. It should be noted that persecution of the Jews in Russia and other communist countries continues to this day.

None of the Jews' persecutions even came close to the evils they suffered under Adolph Hitler and the Nazis. Of the sixteen million Jews living throughout the world at the outset of World War II, only ten million survived. The ghettos, gas ovens and concentration camps are forever burned into the consciousness of the Jewish people. One can only recall the prophetic words written in Deuteronomy:

> Then the Lord will scatter you among all the nations, from one end of the earth to the other. There you will worship other gods- gods of wood and stone, which neither you nor your fathers have known.
>
> Among those nations you will find no repose, no resting place for the sole of your foot. There the Lord will give you an anxious mind, eyes weary with longing, and a despairing heart.
>
> You will live in constant suspense, filled with dread both night and day, never sure of your life. In the morning you will say, "If only it were evening!" and in the evening, "If only it were morning!"- because of the terror that will fill your hearts and the sights that your eyes will see (28:64–67).

THE LAND DURING THE DISPERSION

In the opening section of this book dealing with Israel's history, details regarding the condition of Palestine at the turn of the century are presented. Other quotes from travelers to Palestine in the last hundred years or so appear in this section under the heading "Life in Israel after the Jews Return."

The condition of the land of Israel declined after 70 A.D., and particularly after 135 A.D. In their efforts to quell two major Jewish revolts, the Romans practically denuded the forests. Fertile fields, vineyards and orchards soon disappeared as so many of the land's care-givers were driven out of the country by the Romans. Things became even worse after the Ottoman Turks assumed control of Palestine in 1517, as much of the countryside became wasteland, swamp, or desolate wilderness. Many portions of Scripture prophetically describe the land during this time:

> I will lay waste the land, so that your enemies who live there will be appalled
>
> *(Leviticus 26:32).*

201

I will make it a wasteland, neither pruned nor cultivated, and
briers and thorns will grow there. I will command the clouds
not to rain on it

(Isaiah 5:6).

(There is documentation that the early and latter rains in Palestine
were unreliable many times during the period of Israel's diaspora.)

I scattered them with a whirlwind among all the nations, where
they were strangers. The land was left so desolate behind them
that no one could come or go

(Zechariah 7:14).

The Lord will bring a nation against you from far away, from
the ends of the earth, like an eagle swooping down, a nation
whose language you will not understand.

They will lay siege to all the cities throughout your land until
the high fortified walls in which you trust fall down. They will
besiege all the cities throughout the land the Lord your God is
giving you

(Deuteronomy 28: 49, 52).

Interestingly, the nation with the symbol of the eagle was *Rome*.

THE RETURN OF THE JEWS (Aliyah)

Some Bible scholars have referred to Israel's return as "the time-
clock of God." Indeed, most evangelical students of prophecy believe that the Jews' return to Palestine is both a prelude to Christ's
second advent and to the Jews' own sufferings during the tribulation
period.

Actually, the Bible refers to the return of the Jews to the Promised
Land on several different occasions:

(1) from the exile in Egypt;
(2) from the exile in Babylon;
(3) from their worldwide dispersion in the first century;
(4) a further regathering by the anti-christ;
(5) a complete regathering at the beginning of Jesus' reign
   in Jerusalem.

THE LAND WAITED THEIR RETURN

With all the prophecies of Scripture relating to the return of the Jews to the land of Israel (Eretz Yisrael), one must be impressed with the fact that during their nearly two thousand-year exile the land never once saw the establishment of any other sovereign government. Though the land was ruled by many nations during those centuries, it was kept by God for His people. Likewise, in all their wanderings the Jews never found any other place to claim as their own. During the early days of the Zionist movement and during World War II, there were serious discussions about establishing a Jewish nation in Africa, but nothing ever came of that idea. "Next year in Jerusalem . . . " was more than just a phrase from the Passover celebration, it was part of the very fabric of Jewish thought.

Hidden in the year of Israel's exile and discovered in the year of Israel's return, the Dead Sea Scrolls' appearance could be viewed as coincidental, but the timing of the coincidence is surely by the hand of God.

WHY IS GOD BRINGING THE JEWS BACK?

There are many today who see the Jews returning to the land of Israel but deny that their return has any spiritual significance whatsoever. Yet even these doubters cannot deny the reality of the return. But why are they returning? That is a proper question for both those who believe in Israel's place in end-time events and for those who do not. Several Scripture references speak clearly on this question. Four, in particular, address both the why of their exile and God's motivation for bringing them back:

> Again the word of the Lord came to me: "Son of Man, when the people of Israel were living in their own land, they defiled it by their conduct and their actions." . . . "I dispersed them among the nations and they were scattered through the countries; I judged them according to their conduct and their actions."
>
> . . . "It is not for your sake, O house of Israel, that I am going

to do these things, but for the sake of my holy name, which you
have profaned among the nations where you have gone."

"For I will take you out of the nations; I will gather you from
all the countries and bring you back into your own land"
(Ezekiel 36:16–17, 19, 22, 24).

The second passage relates to Ezekiel's vision of the valley of dry
bones:

Then he said to me: "Son of man, these bones are the whole
house of Israel. They say, 'Our bones are dried up and our hope
is gone; we are cut off.' Therefore prophesy and say to them:
'This is what the Sovereign Lord says: O my people, I am going
to open your graves and bring you up from them; I will bring
you back to the land of Israel. Then you, my people, will know
that I am the Lord, when I open your graves and bring you up
from them. I will put my Spirit in you and you will live, and
I will settle you in your own land. Then you will know that I
the Lord have spoken, and I have done it, declares the Lord' "
(Ezekiel 37:11–14).

The third passage is a word of the Lord to Israel before they took
possession of the land:

After you have had children and grandchildren and have lived
in the land a long time — if you then become corrupt and make
any kind of idol, doing evil in the eyes of the Lord your God
and provoking him to anger, I call heaven and earth as a witness against you this day that you will quickly perish from the
land that you are crossing the Jordan to possess.

The Lord will scatter you among the peoples, and only a few
of you will survive among the nations to which the Lord will
drive you. There you will worship man-made gods of wood
and stone which cannot see or hear or eat or smell. But if from
there you seek the Lord your God, you will find him if you look
for him with all your heart and with all your soul.

When you are in distress and all these things have happened to
you, then in later days you will return to the Lord your God and

obey him. For the Lord your God is a merciful God; he will not abandon or destroy you or forget the covenant with your forefathers, which he confirmed to them by oath

(Deuteronomy 4: 25-31).

The final passage is long and detailed, but these few quotes are in context and speak with great clarity:

"The days are coming," declares the Lord, "when I will bring my people Israel and Judah back from captivity and restore them to the land I gave their forefathers to possess," says the Lord.

"In that day," declares the Lord Almighty, "I will break the yoke off their necks and will tear off their bonds; no longer will foreigners enslave them. Instead, they will serve the Lord their God and David their king, whom I will raise up for them."

"Though I completely destroy all the nations among which I scatter you, I will not completely destroy you. I will discipline you but only with justice; I will not let you go entirely unpunished"

(Jeremiah 30: 3, 8-9, 11).

From these and hundreds of other passages of Scripture, it is clear that God sent the people of Israel into exile because their actions and conduct violated the covenant of the Law. They were sent out to be disciplined and punished. They are being returned because God is faithful to remember His covenant with Abraham, Isaac, Jacob and David. It is not for Israel's sake but for the sake and Name of the Lord.

LIFE IN ISRAEL AFTER THE JEWS RETURN

Scripture has always linked the return of the Jews to Israel with the restoration of the land itself. While Israel was in exile, the land was in travail, much in the same manner as the whole of creation is now in travail after the Fall of Man. Paul's consideration of this truth involving the earth could be applied to Israel as well:

I consider that our present sufferings are not worth comparing with the glory that will be revealed in us. The creation waits in eager expectation for the sons of God to be revealed. For the creation was subjected to frustration, not by its own choice, but by the will of the one who subjected it, in hope that the creation itself will be liberated from its bondage to decay and brought into the glorious freedom of the children of God. We know that the whole creation has been groaning as in the pains of child birth right up to the present time

(Romans 8:18–22).

Surely the land of Israel waited the return of the exiles and her own restoration. The miracle of the land's restoration is visible to all who visit Israel today. Once a swampy wasteland, the Valley of Jezreel has become the "bread basket" of Israel. Yields per acre in that region are among the highest in the world. Is this but another coincidence or has it just happened through the toil of the Zionists? The Bible has its own answer:

. . . "I will resettle your towns, and the ruins will be rebuilt. The desolate land will be cultivated instead of lying desolate in the sight of all who pass through it. They will say, "This land that was laid waste has become like the garden of Eden; the cities that were lying in ruins, desolate and destroyed are now fortified and inhabited." Then the nations around you that remain will know that I the Lord have rebuilt what was destroyed and have replanted what was desolate. I the Lord have spoken and I will do it'

(Ezekiel 36:33–36).

In light of this prophecy, consider the words of Harry Emerson Fosdick when he visited Palestine in the 1920s:

Dr. Weizmann, the supremely influential figure in Zionism, said to me in Jerusalem that for the movement to succeed it was necessary both to remake the people and to remake the land. That is succinct truth. To make Jews into farmers, which is alien to all their history, and to make Palestine profitably arable- these two colossal tasks the Zionists have undertaken. No colony founded since the war has yet become self-supporting. . . . The head of the Zionist Executive in Palestine told me that in half a century (this was 1925) he expected two and a half million Jews to be settled there. Personally, I cannot see where he is going to put them."

In 1988 there are nearly three and a half million Jews in Israel, with an open door for more to come.

Consider also this commentary by Mark Twain regarding an area just north of the Sea of Galilee, after he had visited Israel late in the last century:

> There is not a solitary village throughout its whole extent- not for thirty miles in either direction. There are two or three small clusters of Bedouin tents, but not a single permanent habitation. One may ride ten miles thereabouts and not see ten human beings. To this region one of prophecies is applied, 'I will bring the land into desolation; and your people which dwell there shall be astonished at it. And I will scatter you among the heathen, and I will draw out a sword after you; and your land shall be desolate and your cities waste.' No man can stand here by deserted Ain Millahah and say the prophecy has not been fulfilled.

Other comments by Mark Twain from his 1867 visit to Palestine reveal these impressions of the land:

> . . . a desolate country whose soil is rich enough, but is given over wholly to weeds- a silent mournful expanse. . . . A desolation is here that not even imagination can grace with the pomp of life and action. . . . We never saw a human being on the whole route. . . . There was hardly a tree or a shrub anywhere. Even the olive and the cactus, fast friends of a worthless soil, had almost deserted the country.

These amazing quotes are from an avowed agnostic who was visually impressed with the undeniable fulfillment of prophecies, not regarding Israel's restoration, but regarding its devastation. One can only wonder what Mr. Twain would think of prophetic fulfillment in Israel if he could see the land today.

Other Scriptures which speak about life and conditions in Israel following the return of the Jews include:

> "The days are coming," declares the Lord, "when the reaper will be overtaken by the plowman and the planter by the one

treading grapes. New wine will drip from the mountains and flow from all the hills. I will bring back my exiled people Israel; they will rebuild the ruined cities and live in them. They will plant vineyards and drink their wine; they will make gardens and eat their fruit. I will plant Israel in their own land, never again to be uprooted from the land I have given them," says the Lord your God

(Amos 9:13–15).

This is what the Lord Almighty says: "Once again men and women of ripe old age will sit in the streets of Jerusalem, each with cane in hand because of his age. The city streets will be filled with boys and girls playing there"

(Zechariah 8:4–5).

The words of this prophecy are affixed to a wall in the newly refurbished Jewish Quarter of the Old City. For two successive years, beneath the plaque containing these words, I have seen Israel's elderly sitting on benches while children played in the nearby street.

Jeremiah 31:39 contains a prophecy regarding the building of an extension to Jerusalem. The area described is now part of western Jerusalem. Isaiah 35 tells of the "desert blooming and streams in the desert." The Negev area of Israel, once wasteland, is now alive with flowers and crops. This has been made possible through Israel's national water carrier which brings water to the desert from the Sea of Galilee. So many flowers are raised in the Negev that in the winter months they are exported to Amsterdam for auction in the flower market.

THE REBUILDING OF THE TEMPLE

There is only one city in the world where the Temple of God has ever stood—Jerusalem. There is only one place in Jerusalem which has been consecrated for the Temple—Mount Moriah. Throughout all the centuries following the Temple's destruction in 70 A.D., the thirty-five acre Temple Mount has remained intact, ready to host the third Temple. The preservation of the Temple Mount is an amazing fact, considering the value and importance of land within Jerusalem's walls, and considering the many foreign powers which have controlled the city with little regard for the holiness of the site.

There are three primary questions regarding the Temple and end-times prophecy- Will the Temple be rebuilt? When will the Temple be rebuilt? Who will rebuild the Temple? Today these questions are debated among Christian and Jewish students of prophecy. I emphasize *Jewish* students of prophecy as well as Christian for a very good reason- It is the Jews who will rebuild the Temple. What they are presently thinking and saying on this matter is of great importance.

Will the Temple be rebuilt? There is a general consensus among conservative Christian and Jewish scholars that the Temple will be rebuilt, but when and by whom are keenly debated topics. Some Christian scholars believe that the Temple will be rebuilt before the rapture of the church and the tribulation. Others believe that the Temple will be rebuilt at the start of the tribulation. Still others believe that Jesus will erect the Temple when He comes to reign during the millennium. Interestingly, the same differing views of the Temple's rebuilding are being debated among the Jews in reference to the Messianic age. Which of these views, if any, is correct?. Some scholars, including myself, believe that there is truth in all three views.

Scripture makes clear that there will be a reinstitution of Jewish sacrifices at the time of the tribulation.

> He will confirm a covenant with many for one 'seven,' but in the middle of that 'seven' he will put an end to sacrifice and offering. And one who causes desolation will place abominations on a wing of the temple until the end that is decreed is poured out on him
>
> *(Daniel 9:27).*

Jesus quotes this passage in His Mount Olivet discourse:

> So when you see standing in the holy place 'the abomination that causes desolation' spoken of through the prophet Daniel— let the reader understand—then let those who are in Judea flee to the mountains
>
> *(Matthew 24:15-16).*

Even a literal interpretation of these passages does not insist that a fully restored Temple is essential to the fulfillment of this prophecy.

Though Daniel speaks of the desecration "on a wing of the temple," Jesus refers to it as "standing in the holy place." The entire Temple area is holy to the Jews. Should they have some place of worship on the Temple Mount, it could be the place mentioned in both of these prophecies.

Many Jewish leaders have recently been pressing the government of Israel to permit the Jews to have a place of prayer on the Temple Mount. If granted, this place would surely lead to broader expressions of worship. According to Rabbi Sholomo Goren, quoted in the *Jerusalem Post*, April 20, 1988, Jewish sages held that, even with the Temple destroyed, it was permissible to offer sacrifices at the Temple site. Rabbi Goren, one of Israel's chief rabbis, personally believes that the Jews should have a place of prayer on the Temple Mount, and he supports the idea of rebuilding the Temple.

In the Six Day War, Rabbi Goren was Chief Chaplain to the Israeli Defense Forces. He was present when the Western Wall and Temple Mount were liberated, and said of the event:

> As soon as we entered the Temple Mount, I appointed Jewish officers to take charge of the area. As Chief Chaplain to the IDF, I was in charge of all the holy places. We daily opened and closed the gates of the Temple Mount, entered where we desired and prayed when and where we wished, until the minister of defense, the late Moshe Dayan, stopped us from doing so. If it were not for that, there would today be a permanent place of prayer for the entire Jewish people in the areas of the Temple Mount that Halacha permits us to enter after immersion in a ritual bath (mikveh). We prayed under the open sky in the halachically permissible places, and we could have continued to do so without hurting the Moslems one bit.

The Halacha mentioned by Rabbi Goren is a collection of authoritative opinions by the recognized scholars of Judaism.

The existence of a Temple at the time of Christ's millennial reign in Jerusalem is affirmed several times in Scripture, especially in the book of Ezekiel, chapters 40–48. Regarding the Temple, Ezekiel quotes the Lord:

Son of man, this is the place of my throne and the place for the soles of my feet. This is where I will live among the Israelites forever

(Ezekiel 43:7a).

The dimensions for the Temple described by Ezekiel exceed the dimensions of the present Temple Mount by thirty-six times. The very land around Jerusalem would have to be altered dramatically in order for the Temple of Ezekiel to be built. It is possible that at the time of the tribulation the Jews will either have a "worship place" on the Temple Mount or that some lesser Temple will be erected. Then, when the Messiah comes, He will build the Temple described by Ezekiel.

Since the Jews themselves presently are debating this issue of rebuilding the Temple, it seems appropriate to consider what they are saying. In the April 20, 1988, edition of the Jerusalem Post, Rabbi Goren relates how the Jewish community is divided over this issue. Some believe that the Messiah will build the Temple when He comes. Others, including Rabbi Goren, believe that it is permissible now to build some type of "interim Temple," and that such would not preclude the building of the Temple by the Messiah. In consideration of this idea, Rabbi Goren quotes the Halacha's five prophetic requirements before the Jews can enter the Third Temple period. They are as follows:

1. The liberation of Eretz Yisrael by the Jewish people from foreign domination.
2. The establishment of a sovereign Jewish government.
3. The ingathering of the exiles, resulting in a Jewish majority in the Land and the settlement of most of the land by Jews, though the majority of the Jewish people might remain in the Diaspora.
4. The establishment of the Sanhedrin, the supreme court prescribed by Halacha, without which certain states of the Messianic Age cannot be fulfilled.
5. The building of the Temple.

Rabbi Goren acknowledges the fulfillment of the first three requirements and wonders why all five may not be fulfilled *before* the Messiah comes. Rabbi Goren further maintains that, according to the Jerusalem Talmud, "the Temple will be rebuilt before the Messianic Era." Rabbi Goren's article in the *Jerusalem Post* concluded with these thoughts:

> According to the Jerusalem Talmud, we are permitted to rebuild the Temple and re-establish the Kingdom of Israel, thereby preparing ourselves for the third historical period, the period of the Prophet Ezekiel and his Temple. May it be built in our days with God's help.

These comments from one of Israel's chief religious authorities give cause for deep reflection as they relate to Scripture's own prophetic expressions of the Temple in the last days.

An important question relating to the rebuilding of the Temple is this- *Must the Dome of the Rock come down in order for the Temple to go up?* This question and its implications have bothered many people for years, especially the Moslems. Most conservative Christians scholars have concluded that the Moslem shrine must go, not certain whether a war, an earthquake or some other act of God or man would be required to remove the Dome of the Rock.

Now there are scholars and religious authorities who believe that the Temple did not stand on the location of the Dome of the Rock but several yards to the north of it. Their conclusions are based chiefly on the location of the Eastern Gate which was in a direct line with the entrance to the Temple itself. The perfect alignment of the Eastern Gate with the inner gates leading to the Holy of Holies permitted the sunrise above the Mount of Olives to shine into the Temple through the open gates. If these conclusions are accurate, there is nothing in that area of the Temple Mount to prevent the construction of the Temple.

THE MESSIAH TO REBUILD THE TEMPLE

> Here is the man whose name is the Branch, and he will branch out from his place and build the temple of the Lord. It is he who will build the temple of the Lord, and he will be clothed with

majesty and will sit and rule on his throne. He will be a priest on his throne

(Zechariah 6:12-13).

This passage seems to support the view that Ezekiel's Temple will be built during the millennial reign of the Lord. This reign from Jerusalem's Temple is considered further in Psalms 24, 46, 47, 48; Isaiah 2: 2–4; Isaiah 4:2–6; Isaiah 24:23; Micah 4 and Revelation 20.

We note that, according to Revelation, when the millennial reign of Christ is ended and the new heaven and the new earth are set in place along with the heavenly Jerusalem, there will be no Temple.

I did not see a temple in the city, because the Lord God Almighty and the Lamb are its temple

(Revelation 21:22).

If one accepts an interpretation of the various biblical prophecies which foretell of a Temple built at or before the tribulation and another Temple built during the millennial reign of Christ, the historical account would be as follows:

1. The Tabernacle
2. Solomon's Temple
3. Post-Babylon Temple
4. Herod's Temple
5. Tribulation Temple
6. Millennial Temple
7. (No Temple) The Lord and the Lamb are the perfect, eternal Temple.

THE PROPHECY OF THE CLOSED GATE

Centuries ago, Ezekiel wrote:

Then the man brought me back to the outer gate of the sanctuary, the one facing east, and it was shut. "This gate is to remain shut. It must not be opened; no one may enter through it. It is to remain shut because the Lord, the God of Israel, has entered through it"

(Ezekiel 44:1-2).

This gate, the Eastern or the Golden Gate, has been sealed shut since 810 A.D. without valid reason or justification other than this prophecy.

THE PROPHECY OF WATER FROM THE TEMPLE

There is a prophecy in Ezekiel 47 regarding the flow of water from the Temple to the Dead Sea. These waters will restore the Dead Sea to such an extent that "fishermen will stand along the shore, from Ein Gedi to Ein Eglaim." The same prophecy describes fruit trees of all kinds growing on both banks of the river and continuously bearing fruit (12). A similar prophecy is found in Zechariah 14:

On that day his feet will stand on the Mount of Olives, east of Jerusalem, and the Mount of Olives will be split in two from east to west , forming a great valley, with half of the mountain moving north and half moving south. . . . On that day living water will flow out from Jerusalem, half to the eastern sea and half to the western sea, in summer and winter

(verses 4 and 8).

Today in Israel, the scientists tell us that there is a fault extending from the Temple Mount to the Mount of Olives and beyond. The stage is surely set for the splitting of the Mount of Olives and the living water's flow.

JESUS TO RETURN TO THE MOUNT OF OLIVES

Jesus ascended into heaven from the Mount of Olives forty days after His Resurrection. As He was being lifted out of the sight of His disciples, two angels spoke this message to them:

"Men of Galilee," they said, "why do you stand here looking into the sky? This same Jesus, who has been taken from you into heaven, will come back in the same way you have seen him go into heaven"

(Acts 1:11).

Just as Jesus ascended into heaven from the Mount of Olives, so He shall return to the Mount of Olives according to the prophet Zechariah (l4:4).

THE MESSIAH REIGNS IN JERUSALEM

"Shout and be glad, O Daughter of Zion. For I am coming, and I will live among you," declares the Lord. "Many nations will be joined with the Lord in that day and will become my people. I will live among you and you will know that the Lord Almighty has sent me to you. The Lord will inherit Judah as his portion in the holy land and will again choose Jerusalem"
(Zechariah 2:10–12).

In the last days the mountain of the Lord's temple will be established as chief among the mountains; it will be raised above the hills, and peoples will stream to it.

. . . The law will go out from Zion, the word of the Lord from Jerusalem
(Micah 4:1-2).

THE MESSIAH JUDGES IN THE VALLEY OF JEHOSHAPHAT

In those days and at that time, when I restore the fortunes of Judah and Jerusalem, I will gather all nations and bring them down to the Valley of Jehoshaphat. There I will enter into judgment against them concerning my people Israel . . .
(Joel 3:1-2).

THE MESSIAH IS COMING SOON

"Behold, I am coming soon! My reward is with me, and I will give to everyone according to what he has done. I am the Alpha and the Omega, the First and the Last, the Beginning and the End. "Blessed are those who wash their robes, that they may have the right to the tree of life and may go through the gates into the city. Outside are the dogs, those who practice magic

216

arts, the sexually immoral, the murderers, the idolaters and everyone who loves and practices falsehood. "I, Jesus, have sent my angel to give you this testimony for the churches. I am the Root and the Offspring of David, and the bright Morning Star."

The Spirit and the bride say, "Come!" And let him who hears say, "Come!" Whoever is thirsty, let him come; and whoever wishes, let him take the free gift of the water of life

(Revelation 22:12–17).

There are many people who have seen the *land* of Israel but have never met the Savior of the world. Being bound for Israel does not mean that a person is bound for heaven. Whether your pilgrimage to the land of the Bible is real or imagined, may you know Him "whom to know aright is life eternal." A passport is required to enter Israel today, but when Jesus comes again to reign in Zion, every person who seeks entrance must have on a robe of righteousness, given by the Savior Himself as a free gift of grace.

SHALOM!

Selected Bibliography

Avi-Yonah, Michael. *The Holy Land*. London: Thames and Hudson, 1972.

Collins, Larry and Lapierre, Dominique. *O Jerusalem*. New York: Simon and Schuster, 1972.

Comay, Joan. *The Temple Of Jerusalem*. New York: Holt, Rinehart and Winston, 1975.

Comay Joan. *Who's Who In The Old Testament*. New York: Holt, Rinehart and Winston, 1971.

Dahlin, John E. *Prophetic Truth For Today*. Minneapolis, Minnesota: Beacon Press, 1961.

Dehan, Emmanuel. *Our Visit To Israel*. Israel: Dehan, 1977.

Dullas, John W. *Ride Through Palestine*. Philadelphia: Presbyterian Board of Publication, 1881.

Eban, Abba. *My Country*. New York: Random House, 1972.

Eban, Abba. *Abba Eban, An Autobiography*. New York: Random House, 1977.

Elon, Amos. *The Israelis*. New York: Holt, Rinehart and Winston, 1971.

Fosdick, Harry E. *A Pilgrimage To Palestine*. New York: Macmillan Company, 1933.

Gulston, Charles. *Jerusalem, The Tragedy and The Triumph*. Grand Rapids, Michigan: Zondervan, 1978.

Gur, Mordechai. *The Battle For Jerusalem*. New York: CBS Publications, 1974.

Josephus, Flavius. *Josephus' Complete Works*. Chicago: Thompson and Thomas Publishers.

Kollek, Teddy. *For Jerusalem*. New York: Random House, 1978.

Kotker, Norman. *The Earthly Jerusalem*. New York: Charles Scribner's Sons, 1969.

Laqueur, Walter. *A History of Zionism*. New York: Holt, Rinehart and Winston, 1972.

Levin, Meyer. *The Story of Israel*. New York: G.P. Putnam's Sons, 1967.

Mann, Peggy. *Golda*. New York: Simon and Schuster, 1973.

McBirnie, William Steuart. *The Search For The Tomb of Jesus*. Montrose, California: Acclaimed Books, 1975.

Meir, Golda. *A Land of Our Own*. New York: G.P. Putnam's Sons, 1973.

Meir, Golda. *My Life*. New York: G.P. Putnam's Sons, 1975.

Murphy-O'Connor, Jerome. *The Holy Land*. Oxford: Oxford University Press, 1986.

Owen, G. Frederick. *Jerusalem*. Grand Rapids, Michigan: Baker Book House, 1972.

Patterson, Harriet-Louise H. *Come With Me To The Holy Land*. Valley Forge: The Judson Press, 1963.

Shanks, Hershel. *The City of David*. Washington, D.C.: The Biblical Archaeology Society, 1973.

Thompson, J.A. *The Bible and Archaeology*. Grand Rapids, Michigan: Wm. B. Eerdmans Publishing Co., 1962.

Van Impe, Jack. *Israel's Final Holocaust*. Nashville, Tennesee: Thomas Nelson Publishers, 1979.

Vilnay, Zev. *Israel Guide*. Jerusalem: Hamakor Press, 1972.

Walvoord, John F. *Israel In Prophecy*. Grand Rapids, Michigan: Zondervan Publishing House, 1974.

Walvoord, John F. and John E. *Armageddon, Oil and the Middle East Crisis*. Grand Rapids, Michigan: Zondervan Publishing House, 1978.

Yadin, Yigael. *Masada*. London: Weindenfeld and Nicolson Publishers, 1966.

Yadin, Yigael. *Bar-Kokhba*. New York: Random House, 1972.

Yadin, Yigael. *Hazor*. New York: Random House, 1975.

Index

221